THE
ROSE
THAT
GREW FROM
CONCRETE

THE ROSE
THAT
GREW FROM
CONCRETE

*Teaching and Learning
with Disenfranchised Youth*

DIANE WISHART

The University of Alberta Press

Published by
The University of Alberta Press
Ring House 2
Edmonton, Alberta, Canada T6G 2E1

LIBRARY AND ARCHIVES CANADA CATALOGUING IN PUBLICATION

Wishart, Diane, 1959-
    The rose that grew from concrete : teaching and learning with
disenfranchised youth / Diane Wishart.

ISBN 978-0-88864-516-6

    1. Problem youth—Education—Case studies. 2. Youth with social
disabilities—Education. 3. Teacher-student relationships—Case studies.
4. Alternative education—Case studies. 5. Alternative education—Alberta—
Edmonton. 6. Wishart, Diane, 1959–. 7. High school
teachers—Alberta—Edmonton. I. Title.

LC4803.C32E36 2009   373.1826'92   C2009-902144-7

The University of Alberta Press is committed to protecting our natural environment.
As part of our efforts, this book is printed on Enviro Paper: it contains 100% post-
consumer recycled fibres and is acid- and chlorine-free.

The University of Alberta Press gratefully acknowledges the support received for its
publishing program from The Canada Council for the Arts. The University of Alberta
Press also gratefully acknowledges the financial support of the Government of
Canada through the Book Publishing Industry Development Program (BPIDP) and
from the Alberta Foundation for the Arts for its publishing activities.

CONTENTS

THE ROSE THAT GREW FROM CONCRETE

Did u hear about the rose that grew from a crack
in the concrete
Proving nature's laws wrong it learned 2 walk
without having feet
Funny it seems but by keeping its dreams
it learned 2 breathe fresh air
Long live the rose that grew from concrete
when no one else even cared!

—Tupac Shakur (1999)

PREFACE

"The Rose that Grew from Concrete" provides a particularly apt description of the urban high school in Alberta, Canada, which provides the focus for this book. It is also a fitting portrayal of the students who attend the school. A rose is a climbing plant that can be prickly in places. Its prickliness can often turn away those who don't take the time to notice its more delicate features. Roses grow out of the dirt, and dirt can be, well, dirty. Yet a rose is also fragrant, beautiful, and hopeful. And it can grow in difficult places. So can young people when someone cares to tend to their growth.

At Wild Rose Alternative School (WRS),[1] the students are disenfranchised; they are like roses growing in a nutrient-poor environment. Many are living on the streets when they first arrive at the school, disconnected from their families. All of them are in various types of trouble: drugs, violence, and negative contact with the law. They are in need of a nurturing presence, someone, or perhaps a team of people, who will help. This story, about my learning in relations with students, teachers, and youth workers in an inner-city school, focuses attention on those who nurture the development of disenfranchised urban youth through continuous efforts to soften their prickly spots, allowing their more delicate features to shine. It is also a story of young people who are learning to breathe fresh air.

As an educator, with a background and interest in inner-city school-ing, I was attracted to WRS from the time I first became aware of its presence, located in the concrete shadows of downtown. It certainly wasn't its aesthetic quality that captured my attention. The building is functional at best. It is large, boxy, unattractive, and marginally main-tained. It is cold in the winter and hot in the summer. More accurately, it is cold in some rooms and hot in others. But if it wasn't its physi-cal attractiveness that drew me to WRS, what was it? Something shone through the gloom. It was the people. People working together through drama to tell their stories, stories of pain and suffering that somehow also offered possibilities for better futures.

As part of a peace education conference I attended, I had an oppor-tunity to visit WRS and watch a popular theatre presentation written and performed by students. Highlighting the purpose of popular the-atre, the students gave us a glimpse of their world, one very foreign to most of the audience. We engaged, for a short time, with the students' creative responses to their lived experiences of violence, racism, home-lessness, and of being ignored by the larger society. Yet there was a real sense in the school, a current of hopefulness that intimated: if we could only understand how our stories—those of teachers and youth workers—are wrapped up in students' stories, if we could just work together, here was a school that could help heretofore voiceless young people move forward in their lives.

When I consider how our paths are woven together, how the choices I made are reflected in the choices the youth make, I realize that the journey I have taken has led me to the students at WRS. I have often won-dered why. I have made many decisions along the way regarding what routes to take and the means by which to get to those routes, as well as to various other destinations. I see overlaps in the stories I hear from the youth at WRS as I consider my own difficult youth years, growing up in a home that wasn't quite comfortable. I understand why many youth leave, how the cold, lonely streets often seem a better option. I was never there, but I know the emotions that can lead to street life. I also know about the choices that aren't really choices at all. I chose to stay at home. Many of the youth in this study chose to leave. Their choices were more limited, the option to stay more grim, and the results more desperate. I finished high school, which then gave me more choices and opportunities to take me farther; admittedly, my choices were not limited because of my family's social position and financial means. I chose, and was able, to continue my education, but what of those who had more difficult choices earlier in life, further complicated by a lack of financial and social means to carry them forward? Choices that weren't really choices narrowed to electives unthinkable for the rest of us. Violence, drugs, prostitution, and homelessness become the options for many.

Yes, it was the drama at WRS that initially drew me in. The students' stories spoke to me in a powerful way, a way that couldn't be ignored. From former teaching and learning, I knew that I wanted my path to intertwine with inner-city schooling. Now I knew that WRS was the school for me. In a similar way, the youth knew that WRS was the school for them. It was a school that spoke to them, a school they were a part of. Not only that, it was a school started for them and continually adapted to meet their needs. The images portrayed through those first popular theatre presentations that I was privileged to watch wrapped themselves around my thoughts and increasingly crept into my life. In some ways I saw myself in them. In other ways I was the oppressor, the white, middle-class teacher in multiple positions of authority and privilege. But I wanted to understand the students. I, too, had gone through some of the same emotions and difficulties that WRS youth were going through, but I had landed in a position of advantage, while they were struggling. My empathy for them collided with my desire to understand them and my skills as an educator to engage with them to bring about change.

INTRODUCTION

THERE IS A GROWING awareness across Canada and the United States of the need to improve life chances for young people growing up in poor neighbourhoods, particularly within schools that can give validation and encouragement. The story told here, of WRS, can only enhance our understanding of how schools can take the lead in young people's lives. I believe that this particular population of urban youth, many of whom are Aboriginal, and the pedagogical approach designed to meet their schooling and social needs, can serve as a microcosm for other urban, North American groups of disenfranchised youth. My own journey is bound up in WRS's story, and throughout this book it informs that story, just as WRS helped me to become more self-aware, as a teacher, a researcher, and a member of an urban landscape. Between the two stories of the teachers and students transformed by a new type of school is the underlying, all-encompassing message: there is a great need to attend to disenfranchised urban youth who are currently falling through the cracks of public schools and community services.

Here is an example of a critical pedagogy theory enacted to great affect in the real world. A critical pedagogy works to raise the awareness of students, of their social and political place in the community. In this way, they become subjects, rather than objects, of the world. Students learn to think democratically, to continually question and make meaning of what they learn so as to affect change in their world. We can read until our eyes tear about critical pedagogy "in theory," but there is so little out there about how the ideas play out in a real-life, urban classroom. Yes, as the story in this book will show, the practice is messier than the clean lines of theory, but what in real life isn't? WRS's ability to pull theory into practice, however messy, results in a promising approach to schooling for youth who have not had successful educational or personal experiences in public schools.

Teaching practices are shaped by the relationships formed with those we teach. I have found that I am more mindful of ethical matters in my student relationships when I am teaching youth who have been denied a place in mainstream schools. Teaching at WRS reminded me of my responsibility, as a teacher, to nurture democratic principles in my classroom. Recognizing the worth and dignity of each student means that for some we need to do more to ensure equal educational opportunities.

Urban and educational sociologists point to the many ways urban youth are marginalized in schools and communities. For this reason, in this book I have included the voices of urban youth.[1] As educators search for evidence to support policy decisions related to social interactions in schools, we have witnessed a turn toward objective research. Considerable studies have been done to identify and quantify the social and economic factors that lead to "risk" of not completing high school. This research process demonstrates an appropriate, effective, and replicable method of engaging in research with a disenfranchised youth population and those who work with them. Such research methods have been able to highlight problems related to urban youth and schooling but have been much less capable of identifying solutions. I believe, however, that the WRS story demonstrates the importance of developing relationships in research and teaching, in addition to conducting research to find out which school methods are truly improving the lives of students.

What *The Rose that Grew from Concrete* offers all readers is a snapshot of a particular time and place. We may wonder why it is important to understand this solitary moment when things are so constantly evolving into new forms. The school of this study also, of course, changes continually to adapt to the needs of students. Events and situations I write about here and now may well have sorted themselves into something new and different by the time this book is published. Yet the story informs something more enduring. Illuminating a group of disenfranchised urban youth who have traditionally been unnoticed by scholarship pulls them up and out, brings them into view. It changes the way we, as teachers and researchers, look at them. By shining the spotlight on them as people, they are no longer numbers, statistics, or "problem kids" in the classroom, but real people. These "real people" suggest to us that there may be other real people in our classrooms that call for us to see them differently. Real people who have fallen through the cracks and are struggling. The real people you will meet in this book demonstrate how a rose can grow through those cracks if attentively and patiently nurtured in a school environment.

The ways in which I interpret my story, intertwined with the stories told to me and presented to you, the reader, come from an openness to understanding that is familiar to me and at the same time unfamiliar. The concept of disenfranchised youth is familiar to me. I have, however, had particular conceptions of disenfranchised youth that constantly change and evolve over time as my understandings of both them and me are shaped by time, familiarity, and reflection.

As an adolescent growing up in a small town in Manitoba, I remember a boy, about my age, suddenly appearing in town on a warm summer day. He was cute, personable, and looking to make new friends. It seemed a bit odd at first that he arrived alone, but he quickly pointed out that he was related to a family up the street. They didn't know him, but they let him pitch his tent on their front lawn. I guess they thought his story was plausible enough. A few days later, though, we all found out that he was a runaway from BC, and he was apprehended and returned home.

Thinking back on this experience leads me to think about the historical, familiar concept of the "runaway." A runaway is an underage youth who is misbehaving, someone who has done something wrong and needs to be punished. A runaway does not have parents who have made mistakes but is him or herself the mistake maker. Currently we have "street kids" who are quite literally kids who live on the streets.

xv

Now who is to blame? Well, we aren't sure, but at least new ways of viewing "runaways" mean we don't automatically blame the victims. We now ask, "Why would a young person be on the streets, and what drove them to that cold, harsh place?" But there are other problems that people identify with street kids, especially if they have squeegees! They can be annoying, always lurking about looking for trouble. Upon embarking on teaching and research at WRS, I held particular visions of what street kids were. These visions were familiar to me, comfortable. As soon as I became involved with youth and staff members at WRS, however, the familiar became unfamiliar. My relationships at WRS highlighted tensions between what I understood to be true and what was now disrupted. They opened up conversations that I would now like to open up with you.

Unavoidable in written communication, I have already used familiar ways of categorizing or labelling young people in this book. I have referred to "street kids" and "runaways" and the ways in which these labels focus our attention in a certain way. Perhaps I should explain what some of these terms mean for the purposes of this book, in the context of WRS. As the word "runaway" suggests, the meanings of terms are fluid; we should always define them based on their context, historical or otherwise.

I have identified the group of youth in this study as "disenfranchised urban youth." These young people lead their lives within conditions that deny them many basic human rights, including the right to education. Disenfranchised youth, in this context, are additionally defined as disconnected from families and geographical communities. The discrimination such young people have experienced in schools and within community social agencies has left them cut off from the mainstream of society. Instead, they gain a sense of belonging when they join with peers, forming communities of common experience. The "street" binds them together in time and place. The street is a metaphor, a place where youth come together in a marginalized world that lacks physical and emotional safety.

Because this book presents students as individuals, with individual voices, you will come to know them as single entities. However, labels are necessary in order to talk about these youth as a group.

"Disenfranchised," the currently acceptable terminology in this context, is further defined as lacking a voice, although this is not completely accurate as I have come to understand that these youth do have a voice. It isn't my voice, and it isn't listened to in mainstream institutions, but the youth do speak. Here is an opportunity to listen to what they have to say within the context of an unusual school.

Like the youth in this study, WRS also grew out of the cracks. The institutional field of public schooling in Alberta has left little room for disenfranchised urban youth.

Public schooling in Alberta has changed in recent years, moving away from a more universal mass-education approach. Mass schooling for the working classes in some ways was more effective for disenfranchised urban youth. The idea of greater school choice, indicative of a move to conform to the wealth and wishes of parents, is reflective of current provincial initiatives. Given voice through the *School Act,* it sounds like it should be a good thing. Choice for whom, though, and choice about what? Choice for all, say the boosters, but the choices available are different depending on financial and social circumstances.

The neighbourhood school many of the youth in this study attended and left prior to completing high school is a school with an arts-based focus and a strong reputation for quality programming. Many students want to go there. Those with the *most* choice do, along with the neighbourhood youth who have little choice. This school serves those who not only have the financial and social means to get there but who have always experienced those elements. While there is no school fee per se, art, drama, or dance lessons starting at a very young age would be appropriate preparation for making the choice to attend this school. Knowledge of the social advantages of participation in early training, coupled with the financial resources to pay for it, give middle- and upper-class youth more choices in deciding on which schools to attend. Disenfranchised neighbourhood youth who attend this school, because they live in the area, also have choices. They can leave or wait to be pushed out.

At the same time, the push toward choices in educational institutions has also opened up cracks in the system that allow schools like WRS to push through and thrive. It isn't easy, the obstacles are many, but a rose can grow from concrete. There are publicly funded school systems in Alberta, comprised of both public and Catholic schools. The provincial government also permits both charter and private schools to become accredited and eligible for funding on a per student basis, albeit at a lower level of funding than what public schools receive. WRS is private, provincially accredited and funded. In order to meet the requirements of a private school in Alberta, the school must offer provincial curricula and employ certified teachers, and students must write provincial examinations in core grade twelve courses to graduate. WRS also survives by accessing additional funds from outside sources.

Being a private school allows WRS enough room to breathe so that it can provide flexible programming. However, being "private" doesn't mean that government policy doesn't affect programming. As a private school, WRS is confined by provincial requirements to meet standards of achievement and achievement testing, and the school must be evaluated regularly. Some argue that this framework points youth to "ultimate destinations": choices to pursue further studies at the post-secondary level or move into the workforce. Provincial standards can, however, be limiting, in that school programming has to move in a defined direction. The informal teaching approaches, for example, that work well in the initial literacy program at the school must necessarily fall away as students move into higher-level academic courses. And when teachers are caught up in focusing on the curriculum and preparing students for provincial exams, they have little time for important "student experience" discussions with students that are so valuable to the relationships between students and teachers. Students, too, focus on curriculum content. Years of schooling have taught them that this is the *real* content. It is what is important, what *regular* schools and *normal* youth are doing.

Still, operating as a private school offers the best option for WRS at this point in time, an option that does not require students to pay tuition and allows access to both public and private funding sources. Operating with a formal school structure that gives youth chances to succeed academically and in ways that allow them self-sufficiency throughout their lives is a direction the school has determined to be most effective for the students.

The image of a rose growing through a crack in the concrete is an ideal symbol, not only for the students, but for WRS itself and its teachers. I, too, have grown, encouraged by the light of hope, learning, experience, and close relationships, which nourishes our concrete garden. My learning has been informed by the development of WRS and the people who inhabit it. Like a vine reaching upward, we grow stronger as our stories intertwine. Much can be achieved by believing that a nurtured seed can grow even through obstacles. And from an awareness that boxes aren't necessarily the best place for plants.

Choices in schooling are not as clear-cut and extensive as they might seem. Some seeds can be planted in rich, well-fertilized soil, and the plants that result are carefully tended to. Others are tossed carelessly, allowing the wind to take them where it may. There are better choices available for some, more limited ones for others. My social position allows me to make better choices for my children. Involvement with WRS allows me to see how the illusion of choice affects disenfranchised youth.

The language we use in schools also reflects choices. Documents written to address the needs of disenfranchised urban youth present language that both binds and opens up possibilities. Alberta Education documents, highlighted later in this book, provide an example of this tension. I hope that the language I have carefully used in this book will open up new ways of imagining and understanding the experiences of youth who don't have many choices.

The Rose that Grew from Concrete is based on a case study I wrote about WRS, the research for my doctoral dissertation. I chose WRS because of its unique approach to teaching a specialized high-needs population. I formed my research questions based on my teaching experience at the school and my understanding of how the school worked. My questions also arose from my desire to better know WRS and the people who make up the school's community. There were three basic questions that framed my investigation:

1. What experiences of students at WRS led them to leave public school? How did the intersecting factors of race, gender, and social class affect the school experiences of these youth? What are the

significant differences between the experiences of Aboriginal youth and non-Aboriginal youth within this population of "at-risk" youth?

2. What led these students to return to school at WRS?

3. How does the program at WRS work (theory and practice)? What have been the experiences of students at WRS?

I collected data related to these questions for three months. I interviewed people and conducted focus-group discussions with students, youth workers, early service teachers, and experienced teachers. I wrote the case study with my own teaching experiences in the background, too, of course, and critical theory and critical pedagogy emerged as important influences on my teaching strategies. I found that WRS shares my social vision of an appropriate school program for disenfranchised urban youth. You can see it in the popular theatre and critical literacy foundation upon which the school is built.

I found that researching and writing the case study helped me to develop an awareness of how my power and privilege have had an impact on relations with students even in a school that strives to disrupt power relations. Developing and studying theories of the interpretation and understanding of educational programs in turn help us to understand and therefore change the theories and programs we have always taken for granted.

WHAT FOLLOWS BUILDS on my case study to tell a story of WRS that captures its complexity and uniqueness in schooling disenfranchised youth. In the unfolding, the story reveals and dismantles my own understandings of urban youth and, in particular, Aboriginal youth who may be struggling to find a comfortable fit in urban schools. Through an exploration of student's perspectives, desires, and feelings within the context of schools, we begin to see them as individuals. Tensions of pedagogy are engaged at WRS, and what emerges are practices that offer hope and promise. The experience I share with you is an invitation to shed previous understandings of education for and with disenfranchised youth and to get to know the people who are an important part of the WRS story.

ONE FRAMING THE STORY

I cannot help but see you through my own culture's eyes. I have had the benefit of many kind and patient teachers from among you, and they have done their best, in their gentle and elliptical way, to lead me into clear vision, but my eyes are not yours. I am at least aware that I am largely unaware of your shadings and subtleties, of the real sophistication of your social structures. I will no doubt draw conclusions which you will find laughingly—or insultingly—incorrect. I am convinced, however, that we have no choice but to start talking about such things.[1]

Understanding between persons is possible only to the degree that people can initiate a conversation between themselves and bring about a "fusion" of their different horizons into a new understanding which they then hold in common.[2]

THE STORY TOLD HERE about WRS is only one of many possible stories that could be told about Edmonton's inner city. Some people and groups are more disenfranchised than others in the urban margins— class, race, gender, societal expectations and norms, and combinations of all four, play a part in deciding a person's "place" in any society. This is a story that shows a slice of Edmonton's street life, and many of the possible combinations that dictate marginalization, but it's a different story than those you might hear on the radio or read about in the news because its backdrop is an institution that tries to provide unique educational programs for youth who have been pushed to the bottom of the urban social ladder. WRS is a flagship school, really, a place where teachers have begun to listen to voiceless youth and try to meet their needs, a place that can serve as a model for all schools.

The school is a small, provincially accredited, private, academic- and arts-based senior high school. It gives about sixty inner-city youth the opportunity to earn a high-school diploma and develop skills that can lead to full-time employment and prevent a return to street life. Located in the heart of the city in a community league building, the school struggles to help its students extend the limits of their social reality by teaching them to think critically.

Most WRS students are between the ages of sixteen and twenty-four and have come to the school after having a wide range of academic and social difficulties in other schools. Sometimes the students are coming to WRS after not attending school for a few months, or a few years, and most have attended many different schools as their parents moved from one place to another, and then they took up a similarly transient lifestyle. Many students have had contact with the law. Another thing that nearly all of the students have in common is poverty. Most students at the school live on their own or in group homes. Over 50 per cent of the students have Aboriginal heritage, and many would identify as "mixed race." As well, attending school, any school, has been difficult for WRS students because of personal problems, such as drug use and addictions, homelessness, negative contact with the law, violence, and depression.

WRS aims to engage youth who have left public high schools because of the conditions mentioned above, all of which have made them feel voiceless and mistreated. When Joel, a student, was asked how he felt in public-school classrooms, he responded, "[I didn't like] the way I was treated because the teachers they'd always look at me and...when I needed their help they wouldn't help me and...[I] always had problems in school...[teachers were] always tripping out on me because I don't know...but they didn't have to do that though."

The school's founder and principal developed the WRS program from a unique perspective. His life story is similar to those of his students in that he left school when he was fifteen and subsequently lived on the streets. His love of learning and interest in inner-city youth eventually led him to university to study education. Understanding from personal experience the reality and psychological pressures faced by many inner-city youth, he acquired a formal education that he felt enabled him to help these youth succeed.

Many informal education approaches are incorporated within WRS's programming (for example, involving Elders). At the same time, a structure was put in place that gave youth the opportunity to complete high school and go on to post-secondary studies. The principal knew from personal experience that these youth were not lacking intelligence, just opportunities. Upgrading programs at WRS take place with a sincere respect for the natural intelligence of the youth. For teachers at the school, and everywhere else, "respect" represents an ongoing quest—what does *real* respect look like, and how do we as teachers and researchers know when we have achieved it? Respect involves asking ourselves if all students in our classrooms are provided with the help that they need. It also involves listening to students with the intent of fusing the horizons of our meanings *and* understanding who we are in relation to them.

TEACHERS AND STUDENTS FINDING BALANCE

THE PROGRAM AT WRS is designed to be flexible enough to meet the needs of its students while still meeting the demands of the Alberta curriculum. First-year teachers struggle to find a balance between being flexible and meeting academic standards. As one teacher, Meg, said, "I'm either way over here or way over there. So what works for some kids, doesn't work for others."

How do we see students as specific individuals rather than as abstractions? How do we begin a conversation with youth about meeting their needs while we are already engaged, implicated, and consumed by an educational system that doesn't meet their needs? For example, many students attending WRS receive support money from student finance. Student finance regulations include minimum attendance and academic achievement levels. Students who don't meet these requirements have their cheques withheld by the school principal at the end of the month. Often homework assignments need to be completed before the cheque is released. If not, the cheque must be returned to student finance and the student is generally not eligible to reapply until the following term unless there are medical or extenuating circumstances. Often students are left unable to pay their rent, creating an additional problem for a school that hopes to engage in critical discussions with youth. When the cheque becomes the motivator for completing assignments, moving to a place of critical engagement in learning is much more difficult. As Meg told me, "Some of the kids get so frustrated 'cause they need their money so bad and you demand all this stuff from them 'cause they need their money. It's not 'cause they wanna do it, they're just doing it 'cause they need to get paid."

In addition, being flexible so that students who are having personal difficulties can be accommodated often has an adverse effect on other students who see that "rules" aren't consistent. Meg described one WRS student in the following way: "She [a student] was so worried she was doing all her work and keeping up, keeping her attendance up. She was always worried and then she started noticing other students that weren't doing it and still getting their cheques, so she didn't."

How do we promote *learning* while at the same time requiring students to adhere to accountability requirements of government agencies? As Annie, a teacher, related to me, "I think it comes down to its either intrinsic or extrinsic motivation. Like when you get the introductory kids it's like you have to give them praise and all those other things then it would come to intrinsic and you have somebody like [student's name] who has been through hell and back and she honestly wants to do it for herself. The girl's got a hundred and fifty two credits. Why is she doing that? Because she wants to learn. She wants to be here."

Another teacher, senior staff member James, framed the motivation problem as one of building confidence through academic success. "It's common to the students that we have, a lot of them haven't experienced academic success. And a lot of them are really smart but they just, for whatever reason, missed school. Other concerns with their lives...so the literacy program attempts to play with subject matter that is of interest to the youth...that they can gain success."

Here is an expression of a desire to build a critical approach to learning, but certainly in this inner-city context the possibilities for critical learning are fraught with challenges that come with meeting the more immediate needs of urban youth. And so, at WRS, teachers must accommodate students in different ways.

The formal education system assumes a certain kind of student, that is, a student who does not experience the level of difficulties faced by disenfranchised youth in their personal lives. At WRS, it seems, we try to build a bridge between two cultures of pedagogical approach. Enacting a critical pedagogy within a formal education system is akin to attempting to place a square peg in a round hole. Perhaps, within the school, we must teach the pedagogical conflicts themselves. Exploring such issues within a critical framework may provide answers to the rest of us about how to proceed.

Stephen Brown agrees with the practice of teaching about teaching models in order to find out the best way to teach. To this end, he looked at the pedagogical implications of the local cultural conflicts associated with the environment and with schooling on the Athabascan Indian Reservation in Alaska.[3] Brown explored these conflicts in the classroom; the students, thus, acquired both academic and critical prowess. Perhaps the conflicts that need to be explored initially at WRS are those that define *success* through differing paradigms. What is important to these students in relation to schooling? For example, how do students define *success*? Are there cultural and gender variations in success as defined by students? We need to explore the ways in which this urban context is unique and how schooling could contribute to a *relevant* education.

These youths' experiences reflect those of others who have lived in adverse conditions of poverty. Tupac Shakur, a rap music icon, who many inner-city youth relate to, as his personal life and music resonate so strongly with their own lived realities, is one such example. Tupac, a young black rap artist, was always hungry for knowledge yet found school deadening; he felt it passed on irrelevant knowledge.[4] In his

5

words: "I'm learning about the basics, but they're not basic for me."[5]
Tupac believed that schools should address the pressing social issues
of the day, that they should help youth confront the schooling and societal discord that directly affect them.

As a teacher in an urban context, learning to be flexible was and is
a difficult process. There is much more than flexibility at issue. Being
effective in the classroom also involves examining one's own beliefs
and values. As a middle-class parent, I encourage my children to do
their homework, hand assignments in on time, use their agendas, provide the "right" answers, and to be on time for school. As a product of a
teacher education program, I have learned to "manage" my classroom,
maintain order (a degree of quiet), insist that deadlines be met, and
impart "knowledge." When I first entered the WRS environment, where
the values assumed by these practices weren't necessarily shared, I
became instantly frustrated. As first-year teacher Meg remarked, "You
don't know where the lines are for some of the rules of this school
'cause they tend to get bent on a daily basis." A senior staff member,
James, reflected on this difficulty, "We're kicking out a lot of the ways
that teachers have been trained to deal with people...their feelings of
well-being come from this authority and we're saying no..."

I understood the difficulties some students had completing homework away from school. Many did not have stable home lives or even
homes. Homework just didn't happen. At WRS, we address that problem by providing class time to complete assignments. But what about
being on time, regular attendance, and the quiet orderly classroom environment? It took much longer before I began to feel comfortable with
chaos and longer still to appreciate the creative possibilities of "mistakes" in practice and the critical reality of messiness. My classroom
teaching at WRS has been a continual experience of change in relation to
my views of what formal teaching is and can be. Ongoing engagement
with students and colleagues has shaped and reshaped what it means
for me to strive for social transformation in a democratic context.

In addition, any understanding I may have of flexibility and messy
practice is further complicated by the awareness that what I teach, the
content, is also not necessarily always appropriate at WRS. While poverty
has adversely affected the vast majority of WRS students, the additional

factors of race and gender also contribute to students' experiences in schools. An analysis of race and gender reveals complexities within the student population at WRS. Similarities amongst the experiences of inner-city youth living in poverty are apparent, yet differences can also be seen along race and gender lines. Tupac suggests that classes on issues like sex education, scams, and religious cults would explore the kinds of problems that disadvantaged youth of all colours confront, but police brutality, apartheid, and racism are of particular relevance to poor black and brown youth.[6] While he is getting at the similarities in experiences of poor youth of colour, certainly these issues are important and relevant for discussions with a much wider audience. However, if we are to link personal experiences to schooling, these issues could frame relevant discussions within the context of WRS programming. So topics, not just approaches, need to be flexible. And we are reminded to keep the positive in mind. The youth represented in this book show remarkable ability to overcome the constraints of their social situations. In this inner-city school you can see many examples of the positive attitudes of young people and their hopeful visions of the future.

WRS programming is designed to be flexible in order to meet the needs of individual learners. However this flexibility often does not consider how issues of culture and gender could be incorporated into goals of academic success. For example, many young women in the school are mothers. Understanding these young women, as they would want to be understood and as they understand themselves, is of paramount importance to teaching and learning. Prior to engagement with this school and the youth in my classrooms, I interpreted the experience of teenage pregnancy as a struggle for acceptance by the outside world. I tended to view these pregnancies sympathetically, assuming the mother would choose differently if given greater options. I now believe it is attitudes such as this that constitute the real problem. I still see young mothers struggling for acceptance, but I now think it is the outside world that needs to change. I think this new understanding informs my relationships with young mothers in school. Challenging negative assumptions about young motherhood involves valuing each woman as an individual in the classroom. WRS accommodates particular needs for childcare and flexibility related to the demands of parenting. As well, critical discussions about the needs of young mothers can change teaching practices. Sara, for example, talked about her childcare concerns: "The price of daycare is kind of high, even with subsidy...but it's okay, like she's well taken care of and she hasn't been sick too many times. If I need to I can bring her here [to the school]." She also considered the difficulties of completing her homework: "It's actually really hard because by the time I get home after school it's about five o'clock. I have to make her dinner, get her to eat, give her a bath, spend some time with her and then try to get her into bed, which is not always easy. And then I'm so exhausted by that time it's really hard to get my homework done. Like sometimes I'll stay up really late to do it but most of the time I have to try to do it at school."

The flexible approach at wrs is helpful in terms of providing time and access to teachers throughout the school day to complete assignments. However, Sara identified other ways the school could address the needs of young mothers by providing opportunities for interaction with other mothers in the school: "I think it would be helpful to switch ideas and stuff...just to have a little bit of support...I just don't have time [to attend a Mom's and Tot's group] right now...there's just too much going on personally for me and plus with school and everything."

The difficulties and time constraints of being a single parent make attending outside support activities difficult. Possibilities for school staff to explore include organizing group activities within the school day for students with children. Or better still, incorporate these issues into classroom discussions. This young woman's comments began to reveal her struggles with the world around her rather than internal struggles. It seemed quite clear she was comfortable with her role and identity as a mother.

As educators we are often complicit with racial, gender, and class codes of conduct that cast urban youth in a negative light, and we neglect to examine our own assumptions about these students. For example, Meg talked about students' adjustments to schooling, revealing assumptions made about what is "normal" and what is a "regular" school: "I think he thinks he can change, too. Like a lot of kids think they'll magically turn that button sometimes and be normal kids and attend regular school."

It's worth noting that these youth aspire to this "regular" model, even though we consider the school they are currently attending is designed to address the *deficiencies* they experienced in "regular" schools. Notions of "normal" suggest we are not valuing these youth and what they have to offer. Teachers need to evaluate their own assumptions so they can participate in change. Without this self-evaluation, young people continue to be subjected to schooling that defines and informs their thoughts and feelings from the outside-in, rather than validating the ways students would want to define themselves.

A critical classroom practice supports teachers in evaluating their assumptions. Within my own practice, for example, I reflected on the presence of so many young Aboriginal parents in my classrooms. Young Aboriginal women are living with spouses and/or having babies at younger ages than non-Aboriginal women. I wondered if this was a result of the disproportionate numbers of Aboriginal youth who are disenfranchised and living in poverty. I supposed that if given better socioeconomic living conditions they would not choose to be teenage parents. As time went on, though, I began to question my assumptions. Possibly there were other reasons behind these choices. At this pivotal moment, when you start to question your thoughts and feelings, you need to engage in discussion. I needed to talk to both Aboriginal and non-Aboriginal students. My own experience tells me that if I weren't wholly cognizant of my earlier-held beliefs, I would not be aware of the need for the discussion.

Many Aboriginal parents continually cope with the legacy of colonialism, institutional racism, and poverty. Strong family values are inherent within Aboriginal cultures. I began to wonder how these values contribute to desires to establish a family. I wondered if starting a family at a young age wasn't also precipitated by the disintegration of the families these young Aboriginal parents grew up in and a desire to create something better for their own families. It seems possible that early age of motherhood may reflect a cultural value for these girls, and disconnections from school may contribute to the choices they make.

Strong ties to community are also central components of Aboriginal cultures. In a study in Phoenix, activist Aboriginal women felt

9

uncomfortable about identifying with feminism because it prevented them from feeling like they were full members of Aboriginal communities.[7] Given that identification with community is an important element of self-awareness, reconnections to communities for the young women at WRS need to be fostered. But before anything can happen, discussion needs to occur with those central to the story. In her discussion of Native womanhood, Kim Anderson points out that tribes see woman variously, but they do not question the power of femininity.[8] She goes on to say the gendered nature of tradition can be extremely damaging if interpreted from a Western patriarchal framework. This thought about interpretation suggests to me that, as a teacher, I was projecting detrimental images onto the very students I hoped to help through emancipatory classroom practice. Positive changes in understanding only occur when we begin to see how other cultural beliefs are apparent and relevant in our classrooms. In this case, if we understand woman as sacred life-giver and children as sacred gifts from the Creator, then the perception of teenage pregnancy changes substantially.

Individuals hold multiple perspectives, beliefs, and desires that are always forming and reforming. The young Aboriginal people in this book are unique individuals occupying a particular time and place. As such, we need to get to know them in classrooms in order to truly understand them. All of the youth in this study occupy spaces at the margins of society and can offer a perspective from which to consider the complexities of difference. These multiple points of view are so important to understanding those of varied histories who have come together under adverse conditions on the streets of inner-city Edmonton. Teachers and students can only find balance with each other when they set aside assumptions and engage in discussion.

VALUES AND "VICTIMS"

THE NEED TO RECOGNIZE values and beliefs is complicated because some of those values need to be promoted in order to advance academic success. On the one hand we are recognizing the importance of appreciating the values of others, while on the other we think that some of those values need to be supplanted by our own beliefs. It is not always easy to recognize when we, as teachers, are pushing our beliefs on our students. During my work on the case-study, a teacher, James, talked to me about the need to promote values more conducive to academic success while balancing this approach with the need to increase confidence: "We try to build confidence, from an introductory program that is designed to address problems of literacy and numeracy that most youth [at WRS] have. At the same time we try to instill attitudes that will lead to academic success, like, if you want to get through school you have to come to school; and co-operation, respect for others, non-violence; most youth are used to dealing with conflict in violent ways. We try to show them that isn't always the best plan."

An ongoing struggle is presented in James's words. Building confidence seems to require valuing the students' knowledge, primarily a street-wise knowledge. The attitudes needed for school success, however, are in direct contrast with the knowledge street youth have when they come to WRS. Teachers are flexible, giving students many chances to complete homework, start and restart their programs, and work on behaviours conducive to formal schooling. But how flexible should teachers be? How many chances should students be given? Young people also need to learn to take responsibility for their actions. Yet taking responsibility means adhering to the norms of broader society, a society that has rejected these youth, who have in turn rejected it and its norms. Teachers and students must somehow find the value in both norms: those of mainstream society, and those that the students adhere to. Tupac claims he escaped to the streets from the unimaginative transmission of information in schools.[9] If this is true for the students in this study, then the values we seek to foster, the ones that lead to academic success, are irrelevant to the very youth we hope to place on the path *to* success.

Just being aware of the difficulty presented by this apparent clash in values is a beginning point for reconciliation through discussion. This dialogue needs to be engaged in a way that recognizes the tension that arises and the possibilities for learning from the clash in values that is inevitable in the WRS environment. In public-school settings we frame deviance as the failure to obey group rules. Labelling disenfranchised

11

urban youth as deviant occurs through the dual processes of deviance and conformity. These students have been shaped by a dominant schooling structure that has told them they do not measure up to the standards defined by middle-class society. While challenging this notion, WRS teachers simultaneously prepare students to function within middle-class society, helping them to adopt the very standards that had once rejected them. Discussions of this awkward melding of two opposing sets of values, and the power relations within them, can reconcile the tension for both students and teachers. In what ways have students' values been shaped by their experiences, and how might these values help and/or hinder their academic progress? Maybe the answer to the dilemma of which sets of values to focus on is really a question. Engaging students in these questions, rather than making decisions on their behalf, is a good place for teachers to start. As critical teachers, we can then reclaim power to be exercised *with* students. If our conversations with students can include an examination of the intersections of poverty, race, and gender, we can shed light on this important question of values. Valuing alternative knowledge in school is conducive to building confidence in students and to exploring critical questions of power and schooling.

To this end, two Aboriginal graduates of WRS, Leonard and Claire, who were employed as youth workers at the school when I interviewed them, discussed questions of valuing contemporary and traditional cultural values and knowledge. Leonard commented:

> There's a huge street culture, which is in turn gang culture, which is in turn hip hop culture...they combine elements of Native culture into the hip hop culture...I agree with it but at the same point in time I don't... at least they're taking an interest and they're getting themselves off the streets...and doing something positive to present a message...but they're not going to grow up knowing their total culture...like what about the sweetgrass ceremonies and the smudges and the sweat lodges. Are they going to learn that or are they going to learn to write raps and you know, spin on their head...?

Here are some of the complexities of contemporary urban culture for Aboriginal youth. Culture, as practiced by these inner-city youth, takes on a variety of forms that grow out of lived experience. Questions about traditional and contemporary forms of cultural practice could inform classroom discussions of issues such as poverty, race, and gender.

At the same time, Claire talked about her brother and what she saw as his positive engagement with hip hop: "He enjoys music and has recently taken an interest in the hip hop culture. And in himself and his own Native culture, which he never really touched on before because of the racism that he felt, plus he's gay. He's...producing rap songs that he 13 writes himself that are influenced by his Native culture, by hip hop culture, and by the gay community." Claire went on to say that she viewed her brother's form of expression as positive, enabling him to voice his hybrid identity.

When we don't engage in discussions about difference, we validate some values and ignore others. How might we come to appreciate difference and understand that our differences enrich us? One way is to challenge static notions of culture that come from historical understandings of power and dominance. We can also consider the ways in which some voices, those that speak from a position of power, have been able to choose which cultural expressions are "appropriate."

It follows, then, that in the classroom we need to challenge the values that are entrenched in the system of colonization that has created systemic violence in Canada. But then another question arises. How do we challenge these systemic problems while encouraging the positive cross-cultural values that youth in this study hold? Leonard, reflected on the misunderstandings we have about one another: "So they're in turn saying, you know, 'Oh you're Native and you're poor and I'm not going to talk to you, I'm going to pick on you.' But then on the reverse side the Native person is saying, 'Well, that's typical, every white man does it,' and then that promotes both sides. That's just feeding racism."

It seems that through critical practice we can begin to accept the values of togetherness that these youth want while exploring difficult questions surrounding the social conditions of their lives.

Alberta Learning's 2001 goals for removing barriers for "at-risk" students include making the high school fit the student, not the student fit the high school.[10] This goal, however, will be difficult to meet if schools are to follow the report's prescriptions for new teaching methods, job-training opportunities, just-in-time remedial instruction, and other supports to at-risk students. It would seem that add-ons or band-aid solutions are easier to recommend than overhauling the whole system to make it effective for all students. This lack of flexibility in the public system led WRS to become a private school. The belief, however, that the school should fit the needs of the students does inform WRS practice. As WRS teacher James said, "We try to individualize a program as much as possible. Most of the students who come to the school have serious issues to overcome just to get here. And we need to be respectful of that. At the same time, manipulation is one of the tools that the youth have used to get through their life and we also need to be mindful of that."

In my own teaching practice, I have tried to find balance somewhere between being flexible enough to accommodate individual needs while minimizing the ways I may be manipulated by those who take advantage of this flexibility.

One particular student, Dan, continues to haunt my thoughts, and I wonder if I did what was best for him. Dan struggles with drug abuse. Sometimes drug use has been less of a problem for him, other times more. When I first met Dan, he seemed to have it somewhat under control. He had been attending WRS for quite some time and had generally done well. He had completed a number of courses and displayed strong academic skills. He had also learned how to manipulate people. As his drug problem intensified, his manipulation skills increased. He rarely attended my Social Studies 20 class. Still, I encouraged him to complete the work he had missed. At staff meetings, other teachers suggested that I give him many chances. He never completed much of the work but managed to pass the course. His manipulation skills won out in the end. So what had we taught him? What had he learned about survival in the world? Eventually he took his rent money and bought crack cocaine. His roommate ended up out on the street, as did he, highlighting another complication for students whose financial situations are already tenuous.

The structures of the formal education system, in Dan's case the curriculum, limit the possibilities for social change. I still wonder if I should have been less flexible. Should I have implemented strict deadlines? How could I have kept a conversation going with Dan?

Reflecting on this interaction, I realize I didn't have much of a conversation going with Dan. It seems easier with the students who are new to the school—the ones who can be engaged through option courses, such as photography, literacy, and scriptwriting. The inherent flexibility in these types of courses is conducive to exploring topics relevant to students' lives outside of school. Without a more defined curriculum to get through, we are able to take these life experiences and incorporate students' understandings into reading, writing, and discussions. The more rigid social studies curriculum tends to silence such conversations. Dan, however, needed something other than strict adherence to a commonly understood curriculum. His drug use was a factor that needed to be considered in relation to his studies. Certainly there are many reasons for drug involvement. Often drugs are used as painkillers in order to forget the many problems of day-to-day life.

The provocative street-wise Canadian writer, Evelyn Lau, in her diary of experiences living on the streets in Vancouver, reflects, "What is this pain, that it needs to be obliterated? Drugs have become too important to me. I can't even figure out why anymore, except that the idea of being straight for even an instant is intolerable."[11] Often marginalized youth become part of a subculture where acceptance is conditional on continued drug use. Drug-taking can be an affirmative action indicative of taking control of a situation. This creates another dilemma for teaching in this context. While the reasons for involvement with drugs can inform classroom discussions about power and the lives of inner-city youth, I found it difficult to keep these discussions focused in the classroom. Many students at the school are struggling to overcome addictions and find the topic difficult to discuss. Others may still be involved with drugs, which lead them to frequent discussions about current situations that end up validating drug use rather than getting at the underlying causes of use.

Youth who are currently involved in the use of heavy drugs are asked to leave wrs and come back when they are clean. This practice is necessary because drug use affects their ability to engage with the school and also tends to mean they pull other youth into drug use rather than into schoolwork. Additionally, with drug use often comes a more violent lifestyle that needs to be kept outside of the school. A student named Sara explained, "If you're violent towards another person you have to leave the school. And that makes for a safer environment... for other people. And the fact that you aren't allowed to talk about, like if you went out and got smashed on the weekend, too, because like [name of teacher] always says, there are people here who are recovering from those kind of things and they don't need to be sitting and listening to you talk about that."

Many youth who arrive at the school are still coming off heavy drug use and are occasionally "slipping." Teachers and youth workers endeavour to maintain a safe environment in the school. However, students who are asked to leave are given the benefit of the doubt and are welcomed back regardless of the reasons for why they left. Teachers at WRS understand the difficult life circumstances preceding drug use, and they extend their understanding of student experiences with drugs to classroom explorations. There are so many possible topics of relevance to urban youth within the existing curriculum.

With this in mind, one of the youth workers I spoke to, Richard, reflected on what might be immediately apparent to a new student and the factors that might encourage them to continue attending school long enough for staff members to engage in conversations. "A very different attitude compared to other schools, that's more of acceptance and an effort towards understanding and not being judgmental. Shortly afterwards you realize all the provisions that are being made and the care that's being given when you first walk into the school." Poverty, homelessness, unstable living conditions, and a lack of positive adults in their lives are some of the factors that make settling into school routines difficult for most students at WRS.

Teachers and youth workers endeavour to be accepting and caring in their interactions with youth. Sara explained how important these relations were to her success. "[The staff] were really supportive of me... they always tried to help me even though I was not even really serious about school and they still tried to encourage me...they always take you back, no matter what...I've gone through a lot of shit and it's helpful to have someone that cares about you, tries to help you even though you haven't been as good, the best person or made the best choices...they still accept you and are willing to help you."

Clearly, Sara understood and appreciated that staff genuinely cared about her. But what did she mean when she said "the best person or made the best choices?" When teachers and youth workers strive to be "non-judgmental" are they in fact supporting a belief that some lifestyle choices are preferable to others? While some lifestyle choices are clearly detrimental to the well-being of the young person, I feel that teachers need to rethink the terms "best person" and "best choices," and acknowledge the difficult circumstances in which choices have been made.

In 2001, Alberta Learning completed a study that explored why students left school before graduating and made recommendations that support what Sara said. These recommendations include listening to and supporting students who are dealing with complex problems in their lives. Many students at WRS start and stop the program a number of times before being able to establish a routine of coming to school regularly. One student, Kevin, explained his experience at WRS as follows:

I've been coming here off and on since I was about 15 or 16...I was going to [school name] at the time and then I quit...it was just hard... then I stayed [here] for awhile and I got into some legal problems so I had to leave. That same year I came back again after it kind of cooled out and then went through some more legal problems and I couldn't come back here again. And then I left for a couple years and I came back, this is my third year. So I came back a little while ago and decided I wanted to get my diploma and I want to go to university and stuff so I've stayed here since.

Leonard explained how WRS supports students through many difficult situations in their personal lives. He says that WRS cultivates "a friendlier, warmer environment...designed to make everybody feel like they're safe. Once they come through the doors they shouldn't have to worry about anything else, violence or drugs or anything like that."

17

Students need this safe haven, a place to go where they are accepted and protected from the violence and difficult circumstances of their lives outside the school.

Young people living in inner-city areas are exposed to alarmingly high rates of violence, both as observers and victims. Children living in poor tough neighbourhoods in Edmonton have been shown to experience stress leading to increased and ongoing fear.[12] Violence exposure is linked to depression, substance use, and academic problems. I wonder what we can be doing to build this knowledge into our classroom practices. A safe haven, such as WRS represents, can serve as a "coffeehouse" location for discussions about violence in the community, which I'm sure empowers young people to act in their world.

When we support students and are aware of the difficulties they've experienced with authority figures, we can follow through with new classroom and school practices that further empower students. Youth worker Richard explained one part of school practice that helps to welcome students: "Staff [are] called by their first names; they're not pushing authority on you. They're treating you like a human being, and they're not putting you in a conditional place where three strikes you're out necessarily, but rather one where we give many chances."

James told me about youths' experiences in public schools, saying, "They usually are put in programs or courses intended for behaviour problems because they're not able to meet the standards for school, and as a result they act out, they've poor attendance, and it's just a recipe for disaster."

Then, in a focus group discussion I had with students, Alex expressed his concerns with his public-school experience, an experience echoed by all the youth in the group. Our conversation went like this:

Alex: The thing I didn't like about public schools was a lot more people, that the teachers have less time to focus on you or individuals in the class that need the extra attention...like select, selective students and all that in high schools and junior highs and all that...
Diane: Like certain students get the attention...
Alex: Yeah.
Diane: And others don't.

Alex: Because they do a lot better, or whatever, there's the one person just needs a pat on the back or keep trying sort of thing.

American educator and writer, A. Gamoran, talks about teachers giving unequal attention, pointing out that differences in grade scores within schools are higher than differences between schools.[13] He says that streaming students into separate classes or into "ability" groupings within a class is a significant part of the problem—teachers have higher expectations of those in higher-level groups or classes. When classes are taught at low levels, and with lower expectations, as is often the case in high-poverty schools, students respond less energetically, are more likely to misbehave in class, and less likely to do their homework.

Gamoran's observations support what teachers and students at wRS are saying. However, Alex seemed to have a particular understanding of "select students" who get the attention. I often hear wRS youth point to school size and large classes as reasons for why they couldn't get the help they needed to complete their school work. While on some level they seem to understand that "select students" are not youth who share social circumstances such as theirs, they also don't want to explicitly say so. As James said, "These are not victims that come to us; these are people who have survived situations that would get the better of most of us." ·

My experiences with these youth, both as a teacher and a researcher, tells me that disenfranchised youth do not view themselves as victims and tend not to point out the inequalities and injustices in the world around them. Knowing this has given me pause to think when developing my approach to teaching. Building on the positive strengths of youth in the classroom, when analyzing social structures and talking about positive social action, lessens the dangers of these youth developing a view of themselves as victims.

ENGAGING STUDENTS

Pedagogical moments arise in specific contexts: the social location of the teacher and students; the geographical and historical location of the institution in which they come together; the political climate within which they work; the personalities and personal profiles of the individuals in the classroom; the readings selected for the course; and the academic background of the students all come together in ways that create the specifics of the moment.[14]

AS A TEACHER AT WRS, I have had much opportunity to reflect on how to engage students in academic work. I see struggles both within myself to find appropriate methods to encourage and capture youth in the classroom, and between the philosophical ideals underpinning the school's foundational beliefs and the lack of awareness of the importance of these practices by many of the school's newer teachers. In terms of my own teaching, over time I have developed understandings and approaches that seem to offer possibilities to engage students.

Bridging Courses

The courses students initially take at WRS are intended to bridge gaps between a student's prior schooling and the academic high-school stream they are being readied for. WRS teacher Kristine explained, "We have a lot of bridging courses that can accommodate people individually so that they can get an academic diploma even if they have missed gaps because we have students come here that have missed all of junior high."

These courses utilize drama, photography, video, reading, and writing to explore relevant social issues, while at the same time developing literacy skills. Initially, many students look at the school and surrounding community as focal points for photography and descriptive writing. Theoretically, they then move to examine these objects more critically through questioning and dialogue with other students and staff. As Kristine, said to me, "I think we really try to look at the way of the world, as well as [the ways] the youth that come here manipulate it in order to survive. And I think we look at how they have been maybe manipulated by the world and the structures that they're up against. And we deliberately have elements within our literacy program to help us discuss those issues. Like we'll watch a movie because it's an in to talking about how the world is not a fair place."

While senior staff members consistently use a certain approach in the literacy courses they teach, I've found that, for me, learning to engage students requires careful reflection and refocusing through many blunders and learning from what might be viewed as mistakes. In part, as American educator Rae Rosenthal learned from what she viewed as her own failure, you cannot just put your chairs in a circle and assume you have a critical classroom.[15] I, too, was trying to teach critical awareness in a conventional, hierarchical classroom, and it didn't work. Senior staff members at the school are aware of how this problem impacts on teachers who are new to the school. James talked about how the problem begins in university teaching programs. "The teacher training programs at universities are intended to train teachers to operate in the traditional system...there's nothing that I know of in the teacher training program to prepare teachers to work with a population that we work with...every time we have a new teacher there's a whole learning curve."

And that learning curve is complicated by resistance on the part of the new teachers. They have a preconceived notion of what a teacher should be; a teacher should manage and implement curricular programs rather than develop curricula to fit specific pedagogical concerns. Learning anew requires disregarding many ideas about teaching that are fundamental to teacher education programs and instead developing an understanding of teachers as transformative intellectuals who combine scholarly reflection and practice in the process of critical exploration and learning.[16] For me, the learning curve, while significant, was somewhat shortened by my prior understanding of critical pedagogy and my ongoing academic engagement in topics related to WRS's practice.

While teaching at WRS, I stumbled upon a video that worked well as a teaching tool. Up until that point, I had been frustrated by what seemed to be young people's obsession with Tupac Shakur, whom I viewed simply as a deceased American rap artist. In trying to focus themes on what interested youth, they continually returned not only to Tupac but to the same lyrics and "Gangsta" images. I wondered how to spark some interest in a different topic, refocus on something else, anything else. Then, as I wandered through my local video store one evening, I spotted a film called *Tupac Resurrection*. As I watched it later

21

that night, I realized its significant potential as a critical literacy tool, for in the video, Tupac discusses many issues relevant to the lives of inner-city youth.

When I played the Tupac video in class, it became a springboard for discussion leading to writing. One student, Chantalle, offered that she, too, had written a poem on some of the same themes Tupac had written about, as she had lived through similar experiences. Her engagement with the topic and interest in writing about it created an opening that allowed for and encouraged critical discussion. In subsequent classes, Chantalle continued to write on themes relevant to her life and gradually came to understand how societal structures have had an impact on her experiences. Later in the course, I added current news articles to our discussions. One article, about complaints against the Edmonton police department, led to dialogue about community policing, with students suggesting the police should be focused on helping people in the inner city. Eventually Chantalle wrote a letter to the newspaper, which she hoped would foster understanding about police violence toward disenfranchised youth.

On the second day of our Tupac unit, three new male students arrived. Their presence changed the dynamics of the class considerably. Three quiet female students weren't attending that day, and the new students were loud and boisterous. I was worried that I wouldn't be able to keep the Tupac conversation meaningful. The new students were immediately interested, though, when they learned we were to watch *Tupac Resurrection*. I explained we were engaged in media analysis leading to writing, hoping to promote an understanding of the educational significance. While this overview was at first met with groans and "let's just watch the movie" they were quickly engaged in discussion. The topics covered by Tupac are ones that these youth know much about and are interested in. Tupac talks about his mother's drug use (crack cocaine). Both Braydon and Chantalle responded with stories of their own mothers' drug use. Braydon said his mother uses cocaine, and Chantalle said marijuana was acceptable in her mother's house when she was growing up. Now that she had a baby of her own, she realized she didn't want him to grow up that way and recognized that the drug use around him would be an influence. The discussion was loud and often seemed out of control with more than one person talking at once. It felt uncomfortable for me, as I like more orderly conversation. I understood, though, that I needed to let it unfold and allow them to tell their stories, a process that came to be exciting as they developed an awareness of their shared experiences. My hope was that their willingness to talk about the issues and tell their personal stories would mean they would be willing to write about them, and, ultimately, want to become part of projects to affect positive change in their personal environments.

I gained so many important insights during the first class where we discussed Tupac, and the ones that I conducted thereafter. It is often so hard to explore personal issues and open old wounds in a classroom setting, and the Tupac unit requires difficult emotional work both from me and the students. I do, however, think that the process allows all of us to transform our lives. Certainly my teaching has been transformed through my interactions with them. And the students come away with a self-awareness that they didn't have before; they have recreated themselves by talking about and understanding their own lives in a way they hadn't before. Just knowing that others have experienced similar difficulties in their home lives seemed to make it okay for them to talk about it. They understood they might not be so different after all. It was like they had come to a realization that maybe there was no need to hide it, to feel ashamed about things that weren't their fault. Seeing students remake themselves makes me want to find more Tupac-like units to introduce to the classroom.

I've considered including Aboriginal rap music in classroom discussions because I think, like Tupac's perspective, the various points of view displayed in this music could be incredibly emancipatory. Rap groups, such as Alberta's War Party, make connections between the social problems underlying American rap music and the social problems that inform Aboriginal music. "This is our ghetto," says Omeosoo, or Kool-Ayd the Chubby Cree, as he calls himself onstage.[17] He refers to Hobbema as "the hood," a place that is anything but an idyllic rural setting. More and more Aboriginal youth, especially those on reserves, are equating their experiences with the lives of young people in African American ghettos. The "ghetto" is a world they're exposed to through the mass media, and they're adopting the look and the music of that culture. Aboriginal rap groups are also bridging gaps for an increasingly urban Aboriginal population, giving voice to issues of economic and social deprivation. Rex Smallboy, also of Alberta's War Party, notes that people who have had their pride and dignity assailed for generations are now voicing those experiences and, for him, rap provides that voice.[18] The music has become a healing tool that showed him how to move on with life and have a positive attitude. I believe I could use the opening Tupac creates to move Canadian Aboriginal rap into the classroom as a springboard for discussions about local and personal issues that affect these youth directly. This approach to teaching is, however, far removed from the pedagogy presented to us in teacher education programs.

The Teacher's Learning Curve

When I interviewed senior staff members for the WRS case study and I noticed that they all brought up concerns about the learning curve of new teachers, I held a focus group discussion to talk about it. Wondering how new teachers felt about their transitions from other schools to WRS, I began the conversation with them by asking for reflections on these experiences. One new teacher, Meg, commented, "I'm easygoing and soft spoken but I'm a hard-ass, so it's hard to let go."

This teacher saw the need to adjust her approach, but she didn't appreciate the reasons for it. New teachers do, however, seem to understand the student population and some of the structural violence in the lives of students. As Meg said, "This environment has made me a little more open to people in that situation." When she said "that situation," she meant poverty, homelessness, and drug addictions, but she still seemed to have difficulty connecting these issues to school practices: "I personally would want a little more leadership...maybe a little more for a new teacher...I haven't learned by trial and error yet...and that doesn't make me comfortable. You get whisperings from the other staff of what you can and can't do."

Meg was looking for outside direction that, in a critical approach, should come from within. The idea of critical pedagogy or any understanding of critical practices in the school did not come up in discussions with these new teachers. They seemed unaware of this kind of teaching method.

I tried to discover where the bulk of the teachers' frustrations were in terms of transition courses. It seems that they were most concerned with having to accommodate students who started the program late. As Meg said, "She kinda came in late. I think she came in like right around Christmastime or just after. And she skipped out on all that so, she missed a few steps."

The new teachers know the importance of bridging courses in terms of skill development prior to beginning academic courses. They see that students who have "missed a few steps" have difficulties later on. About a student who seemed to be missing certain skills, wrs teacher Annie said, "She came in and she's got the worst reading skills. We never got a time to actually teach her how to read and understand. We just put her in math and science and cts [Career and Technology Studies]."

While recognizing the value of increased skill levels, these teachers did not seem to be aware that both the content of the curriculum and critical methods of pedagogy partner up to teach students. The new teachers at wrs taught presuming that content, learning activities, and the teacher's role in facilitating the acquisition of knowledge would be sufficient in their new classrooms. They seemed to feel that learning is simply a matter of acquiring curricular content. Given this understanding, it is not surprising that early service teachers at wrs were not aware of alternative ways of learning.

The realty is that teachers need to accommodate youth who come to wrs "late" (in fact at any time throughout the term). Many youth are referred to the school by group-home staff or through the justice system. Their need to be in a program is immediate and can't always be held off until a new term starts, when it would be more convenient from a school-programming perspective. Many students also often start and stop numerous times before being able to establish a routine of coming to school. Some of the bridging courses are set up to try and accommodate this need.

A senior teacher in the school, Kristine, revealed some of the messiness that is inherent to wrs when she explained, "We have it set up so that they can work intensely on a credit, and if you miss a certain amount you can come back and pick up where you were at so it's fairly self-directed. And hopefully there's enough staff so that you can work continuously...and hopefully get a credit. And we do include some of the competency-based computer credits. Which means that if that is a strength for you, you can get credits very quickly."

This inner-city school attempts to overcome the difficulties of students who, in James's words, "consistently will have to take several runs at it." The benefits of a program that provides enough flexibility for these students include an opportunity to experience success. As youth worker Leonard said, "It gives them a sense of accomplishment...a lot of the kids that have come here haven't experienced any kind of success, be it through a job or anything...they complete two or three credits and they're beaming." And, James elaborated, "...the use of the arts is critical in our work because it allows us to address academic deficiencies in a way that allows students to maintain some sense of dignity and self-worth and also promotes their confidence at the same time. We're able to move toward the academic courses and feel good about the whole process rather than putting them into a reading program that highlights their deficiencies."

But what about critical practice? James seemed to say that building confidence through *skill* development is what is important. A focus on skill development seems inconsistent with the goals of a pedagogy that purports to change students' understandings of their place in the world. Certainly we need to build confidence, but it needs to come from an awareness of self and society. I discovered tension between the broader goals of emancipatory education and the narrow goals of skill development in schools.

To this end, here is a question I continue to grapple with in my own teaching: What would an emancipatory pedagogy look like if it were set up to meet the needs of those students with inconsistent attendance? There are times when I am exhilarated to see students connecting with issues and with each other in the classroom. This excitement is always tempered by knowing that I may not see some of these students again, or at least not the next day. I also know that some will continue for a while and then leave and possibly not come back. It sometimes feels like the first day of term every day for a week, in terms of getting to know students. But maybe this isn't a problem. There is creative possibility in new groupings of students, new ideas, new conversations.

There is, however, also a need to build trust before people will open up in the continually changing group. As a teacher at WRS, I have learned that I need to build trust quickly.

It seemed that the new students were willing to share their personal stories on their first day in the school when Tupac's story broke the ice. Did Tupac make it okay? Did I make it okay? But beyond the positive effects of Tupac, I have discovered that the momentary nature of success in this context is reflective of tensions between the roles of teacher and student as they struggle for a culture of democracy. My teaching is informed by an understanding that the tensions are an ongoing and natural part of day-to-day classroom relations. Given that my role as teacher in the classroom puts me in an undeniable position of authority, I consider how to produce a non-hierarchical classroom. What might my students' vision of a democratic classroom look like? How might they have solved the *problem* of too much Tupac? Questions such as these frame a critical discussion leading to paths for exploration of deeper social issues.

Building Relationships

An integral component of being a critical teacher involves initiating and maintaining ongoing positive relationships with students. Leonard reflected on the importance of establishing relationships with youth when he told me, "If I come across being too hard or too firm I stand a chance of losing any rapport I might have with the kids....They've faced so much adversity in their lives they don't know who they can trust."

Beyond initial welcoming approaches, there are some longer-term considerations a teacher or youth worker must think about in the WRS context. Leonard continued, "I'm very open...I tell them, it's only fair... they're letting me know stuff about them, anything they want to know they can ask me...that helps with the trust, too. They can relate to the fact that I had to go through a series of steps through my life which brought me to this point...I can relate to them with their situations."

Leonard gets at the idea that teachers and youth workers are a part of these relationships. It isn't just the students' experiences that are important. Our stories need to be shared, as well. This collaborative approach results in a pedagogy that is concerned with processes and interactions among class members. But how do we move this approach into the classroom to facilitate exploration of shared social realities? Leonard believes he relates well to youth in part because he has shared experiences similar to those many of these students are currently experiencing. Students support this understanding. As Kelsey, a student, said, "Leonard has went through a lot of crap. Like he knows everything that's happened to me in my life and he's just helped me actually stay, like he's actually convinced me a couple times from leaving."

Regarding teachers James and Kristine, Carl, a student, added, "...they all come from fairly rough backgrounds. So they really connect....They know pretty much what we're going to go through during our time here and they're really interested in helping. They treat you like a person."

So what of me and my middle-class background? How do these students perceive me, and do they think I understand them? I wonder if it is just the common shared experiences or is it also the way of interacting that students appreciate. It seems it is important to share one's own story, even if it is a different story. Reflecting on a classroom experience led me to believe that meaning is co-created through this process.

I had written quotes up on the board and asked students to select one to write about. Most wrote something. Braydon wrote a paragraph on his drug use—told me there was a lot more to the story about his family but he wasn't going to write it because it was stuff he didn't want anyone to know. I let it go. In retrospect I shouldn't have. The fact that he told me that much seems to be an indication he might have talked about it in some way. Maybe I should have told him there were things about my family I didn't want people to know about either. Things that are uncomfortable to talk about. Like my father's alcoholism and what it was like to grow up in our emotionally stifled household. A bridge could have been built between his experiences and mine—a platform from which to create new meanings, new understandings—a way to tap the creative potential of our differences. This approach is, of course, contrary to the ways in which teachers are constructed both within teacher education programs and within public schools. It offers a possibility for new beginnings by refusing to replicate existing practices of schooling that have failed to engage disenfranchised urban youth.

Students clearly appreciate, at least with time, the relationships they have with staff members at the school. They point to these relationships as an important component of WRS. They also validate daily sharing circles, a process that is used to build community, make decisions, and minimize power differentials. Kelsey, a student, said, "I like the fact that the students have a say in the school rules and what goes on and what kinds of things they'll be doing, stuff like that. And that the courses are mostly based on what the majority of the students need to know to graduate." Voice, from the students' standpoint, is something they have in daily sharing circles, but classrooms are focused on getting through required course work. The traditional sentiment that suggests voice is not an important component of in-class participation presents an ongoing difficulty at WRS.

Within my own teaching practice, I have made a conscious effort to share and encourage sharing of voices, yet I've often found this is easier said than done. For example, I began one literacy class with a short discussion about respect. Given that we were discussing personal and sensitive issues it seemed inappropriate that some students were talking, laughing, and making rude remarks. What I didn't understand at the time was that these responses might have been a defense against the pain the students were feeling as a result of the topics we were discussing. When I brought up "respect," it should not have been a reprimand or a speech. I had missed an opportunity to engage students in dialogue and listen to what they may have had to say about respect. In retrospect, my failure to capitalize on a teachable moment appears as a lack of fusion of theory with practice—a disrespectful approach to a discussion of respect. In fact, any attempt by teachers to "handle" the class is inconsistent with what WRS students have said they appreciate about the school. Real "voices" in the classroom are needed but difficult to encourage.

The Arts and an Almost-empty Camera Bag

How do we get to this place of shared voice and vision? At WRS, students and teachers find their voices through the arts and the literacy program, which are both used to look at the world around us. Teachers can always better meet the needs of disenfranchised urban youth by approaching students with the knowledge that the students possess diverse social realities and have a right to speak and represent themselves in their learning. Students and teachers should be able to negotiate within their cultural realities to constantly remake their own identities. Through popular media, students can challenge power blocs while creating alternative visions of the world. At wrs this challenge is often approached through photography. As Kristine said:

> digital media and also basic photography...gives somebody a purpose: to go out into the community and look at it. I mean literally looking at it through a lens that you also have something between you and the community and you have a stake there that not everyone else has...once they're given that prop they would go out and really look at the community with a different purpose...they have a role that's valid within the community...suddenly they have a place within the community...and at the same time they're not a part of it. They're separate so they can really look at it from the other side...it gives them a power they haven't had before.

Students use this medium to critique the messages in the world around them and consider alternative representations of the images they see. Photography provides not only opportunities to view the world critically but also allows students to name and talk about the community of which they are a part.

When I think about how this happens at wrs, I remember one incident in particular. I had left in a hurry after class one day and had forgotten to put the disposable cameras away. When I arrived back at school the next day only two cameras remained in the bag. My initial thought was that I had erred in not putting the cameras away, since now some of them were missing. When I think about it now, I can see that I could have looked at the camera bag incident much differently. In the classroom, we are all a part of the community to which the cameras belong. Incorporating this understanding into classroom discussion would have included the entire community in building understandings. I made a mistake when I failed to recognize the almost-empty camera bag as an opportunity for discussion.

This type of error, not a teaching one, per se, can still be illuminating. This incident might have been used as an opportunity to view the world more critically, a teachable moment. What could the empty bag have represented? How might the students have viewed the bag? The cameras were theirs anyway. They were for use in our class by them. The school pays for photo finishing so in order to have their images developed, the students would eventually have to either admit they took the cameras or pay for film developing themselves. Did they think any of these questions through? Is it just that the cameras were accessible, so why not take them? Why do I now think I can't leave cameras unattended? The problem could have been solved in class, thereby establishing trust so that cameras could be left lying about. Developing an understanding of community that placed all of us at the centre would have made cameras the shared property of the class.

I understand that the school exists to meet the needs of urban youth who did not have their needs met in the public school system. This is an important thing, as a teacher, for me to understand. Students, too, need to understand their context differently. Teachers need to impart the understanding that we do not wish to be regarded in the same way that the students regarded their previous teachers. But, what would their side of the conversation about the cameras have looked like? How about the almost-empty bag as a metaphor? Might it frame a discussion about the inner city? What is the message in the two cameras left behind? In what ways could what was left be used to refill the bag? There are so many possibilities in this one incident for framing critical discussions relevant to urban youth.

Urban Intersections

When we start looking through the lens at Edmonton's inner city, we see poverty, homelessness, a disproportionate number of Aboriginal people, drugs, violence, children playing in parks littered with needles, struggles to get by, positive shimmers of light here and there, smiles, and people who look unhealthy to me. A few years ago, my partner and I decided to volunteer, with our children, at an annual inner-city New Year's Day dinner. We were part of the dessert crew. Our children liked this job because it allowed them to hand out candy to the kids and carry trays of desserts to the tables. They find people are friendly when you approach with sweets to offer. I find they are friendly no matter what—there is always a cheery hello.

Even though I have worked in the inner city, I find I learn new things about myself as a result of this volunteer experience. I notice similarities between me and others. For example, mothers who don't want their children to have sweets until they have eaten their meal. Why would I even notice that? Isn't it obvious that children should eat the healthy stuff first? Did I expect something different? Did I think because they are poor they might not hold the same hopes and concerns for their children? Equating "good" parenting with a three-bedroom bungalow in the suburbs fails to recognize historical conditions of colonialism, institutional racism, and cycles of intergenerational poverty.

In Edmonton, many urban families lack the basic necessities of life. Many of these families are included in the 52 per cent of all Aboriginal children in Canada who are poor. According to the Ontario Federation of Indian Friendship Centres, some effects of this poverty are low self-esteem, depression, anger, self-doubt, intimidation, frustration, shame, and hopelessness.[19] Leonard, one of the youth workers at WRS, who grew up in poverty in Edmonton's inner city, talked to me about how he sees the effects of poverty:

> being an Aboriginal myself, knowing how it feels to be placed in that situation, when you're called dirty Indian and you know you see the people who drink out on our benches...and when someone says "Indian" the first thing that comes to a person's mind is a stereotype of what they see out here. So when these kids grow up with that, they perceive that and they come to think that's all they're going to be. So it's almost like they give up on themselves, you know, because they think, "Well, I'm just an Indian anyways, so what's the point."

Leonard pointed toward the process by which inner-city Aboriginal youth come to construct themselves outside of the "norm" of mainstream society. But what is he really saying in these words? Starting with "the people who drink out on our benches." How did they get there? Consider the historical relations by which social conditions and attitudes were created toward people of different cultures and colour, who became colonized in a class-structured society. In creating systemic violence in Canada, we have created, in urban Aboriginal youth, the kinds of understandings reflected by Leonard.

Leonard's comments point clearly to the intergenerational effects of societal restraints on Aboriginal peoples. In schools, we need to consider how to best educate youth who believe: "I'm just an Indian anyways, so what's the point." Teachers need to recognize that critical identity issues are at stake before they begin discussions with Aboriginal youth. A 2002 interdisciplinary study on Aboriginal youth and schooling emphasizes the importance of validating identities and incorporating spirituality into formal education programs.[20] The authors consider how a critical pedagogy framework, similar to that at WRS, would allow schools to reclaim Aboriginal youth who have become disenfranchised. They also examine how a program that is relevant for disenfranchised Aboriginal youth can also be relevant for disenfranchised non-Aboriginal youth of both genders.

Another educational researcher, Fyre Jean Graveline, offers a pedagogical approach she calls "First Voice," which is a tool she developed out of critical pedagogy and Aboriginal discourse for use in her university classrooms.[21] First Voice is the voice of personal experience. Graveline encourages her students to interpret their own experiences, in ways that will guide and inform their knowledge base. First Voice places authority in personal experience and individual identity, and as a critical pedagogy it challenges why and how certain positions are privileged over others. As such, it begins to raise student's consciousness to their own lived experiences and helps students look for ways to change their social reality.

WRS also allows students and teachers to mount the same kinds of challenges, but at this inner-city school a popular-theatre approach to discourse was adopted because it allows inexperienced participants to conduct complex social analysis. Through theatre, youth can explore their own social reality, draw their own conclusions, and work toward appropriate responses. Claire, an Aboriginal youth worker and former student, explained a part of the theatre process to me: "There was a play we did...because the ratio of Aboriginal youth in the drama group

33

was well over the population of non-Aboriginal youth at the time. So we switched the roles in the play where there is a white student that went to a Native school on a reserve or something and they were the ones that were being treated badly."

Issues WRS students explore through drama include racism, violence, and prostitution. These themes emerge after youth examine their own experiences. While drama is used as a healing tool, teachers ensure that students don't end up simply critiquing from a dominant perspective. This critical pedagogy approach offers ways to view the social realities of those on the margins. Paulo Freire, an educational thinker, identifies this process as "conscientization," whereby participants engage in action to transform their situation.[22] This conscientization process, highlighted by the school's drama program, is the process that originally led to the creation of the school. Students, having examined their social situations through drama, identified a need for schooling as a way to change their realities. Drama continues to be an important component of school programming.

Claire continued her reflection on how her involvement in the play caused her to think about an issue from a different perspective when she played the part of a white girl. "We were actually in the play and working on the scene and I thought about my opinion on it and I had to because of the play and there was a girl that was vocal in the play and she was the one who was saying the things about white people. You took our land, took our this and that, and I had no idea how to react to that because that's purely on defense mechanisms."

The dramatic performances often raise issues that require further discussion and analysis in the classroom. For example, would people living on reserves approach these issues differently than those living in cities? In the inner-city neighbourhood where WRS is situated, Aboriginal and non-Aboriginal youth live together. Their lives are intertwined. Because they've known each other for a long time as friends and classmates, they have come to understand one another as individuals. At the same time, Claire revealed the students' need to address historical relations in Canada that continue to affect the daily lives of Aboriginal youth. Both students and youth workers I spoke with insisted that we all need to live and work together in order to work through these issues to attain a point of greater knowledge. They believe we need to understand each other through cross-cultural awareness derived from being together in schools. As Leonard said, "I think that's where the problem is....It's fear of the unknown. You don't know something, something you've never seen before, so automatically your first reaction is to hate it, not like it."

We need to *be* together in order to learn to *live* together. An interesting thought when we consider the experiences of non-acceptance these youth have had in public school settings. Why do they still want to be together? Perhaps the rejection they experienced is feeding a desire to be accepted in an integrated setting. Their beliefs seem to be that we just have to learn more about each other, our history, and our ideas of privilege in order to get along. A popular theatre approach gives youth voice and allows them to develop awareness through adopting the role of someone else—it helps them to learn more about each other. Sara, put it this way, "So that everybody's kind of learning something about other people and also about themselves...the ways that you're similar and some of the ways that you're different and sometimes differences are good things, too."

Financial Considerations and Other Supports

Financial concerns are a significant consideration in a school like WRS. Money consumes much time and attention, and, sometimes out of necessity, overrides programming needs. Lack of adequate funding sometimes hinders the ability of school staff to pursue what they feel are best approaches.

While the school requires cold hard cash to maintain school programming and small class sizes, it also needs material supports for students. Both students and teachers recognize the importance of various supports, such as bus tickets, winter clothing, lunches, and hot showers. James told me, "In terms of supports...one of the supports is bus tickets. Because many youth who come just don't have bus tickets, or don't have transportation or enough money for transportation and they can't come to school. And of course the other thing is the lunches and breakfasts. And we've also done winter coats...damage deposits."

WRS students appreciate the extra supports offered at WRS. Kevin said, "There's a lot of people that can come here that may not be able

35

to eat anything at lunch and if it was like a regular high school they wouldn't get nothing because you have to pay the money in the cafeteria, right? And here they get it for free so it's a good thing and it's always quite healthy."

Carl, another student at WRS, recalled, "I remember [student's name], they used to let him take a shower because he didn't have a shower. He used to come here and shower in the morning, get coffee and bagels..."

Alberta Learning covers less than half the costs to operate the school. In order to meet the needs of students, WRS has to come up with the remaining operation funds, as well as provide additional supports. In addition, WRS provides out-of-school programming for students that fosters a sense of independence and empowerment. The money for these programs that has to come from the community is significant, and gathering it poses a constant challenge. "As the number of students increases, the need for programs and staffing makes the problem larger," said James. In 2005, the school attained private-school status in the ongoing effort to retain flexibility in programming through autonomy, while meeting financial needs. This status has led WRS to a key source of funding: accessing provincial funds for students with special needs.

Special Needs and the Problem with Coding

Many youth at WRS are coded with moderate to severe emotional or behavioural disabilities due to maladaptive behaviours that interfere with learning. While some students arrive at the school with a previously identified special education code, all go through an intake process when they arrive at WRS. It is through this process that chronic and pervasive behaviours are identified—behaviours viewed as ones that need to be changed in order for the students to finish high school. While the practice of coding provides significant funding that can help students learn in the classroom, it also creates some difficulties.

Senior teachers and youth workers at WRS argue this funding allows them to continue operating and even provides some breathing room. Without it, where would these youth be? Possibly back on the streets. But there are problems created by having to "code" for these dollars. The very idea of "coding" clashes with the teaching model the school is trying to uphold.

One student stands out in my mind when I think about this issue. Eric was a new student to the school and had been attending my literacy class for a few days prior to intake assessment by a youth worker. The evaluation classified his literacy skills as very low: early elementary. Eric was further assessed as suffering from depression. In light of this information, I added a drawing assignment as an option for the next day's class hoping to engage him. I identified themes from the Tupac video, such as love, anger, and redemption. Students were asked to draw whatever came to mind about the word(s) they chose. Eric didn't draw much but offered some interesting remarks about the words "redemption" and "adversity." His comments indicated a very good understanding of these words, a strength that required building upon in the classroom.

So, first, how does a youth with literacy skills labelled as "early elementary" develop such a good understanding of fairly complex words? Clearly they are words he is interested in. Where did he encounter them? Through music or poetry? Did he come to understand their meaning through the context in which they were used? Or did he look them up? The intake "tool" used to assess literacy skills is limiting for youth who have learned survival on the streets. These youth possess other kinds of literacies that could be meaningfully measured in order to assess literacy levels.

As a teacher, I, too, was a part of that intake process. My role was to observe students' behaviour and, using a checklist, record behaviours that are inappropriate or hinder learning in the classroom. For example, "offensive language," "open defiance," "argues with others"—all of these are included on the form. During each class I was to indicate the number of times each incident occurred. The form asks teachers to report every incident, however minor. Having to count the number of times some of these youth swear in an hour highlights the absurdity of the activity. Swearing is culturally appropriate within their environment, not indicative of behavioural disabilities! However, the numbers of incidents tallied support reasons for referral and, along with other indicators, determine whether or not special needs funding is granted by the province. We need to highlight the "deviant" in order to receive funding. The positive attributes of these youth are not considered. This process makes it difficult for teachers to focus on strengths, such as the above noted student's understanding of words, when we have to spend the entire class counting the number of times students swear.

Senior teachers and youth workers reject the pathological picture of students as painted by these coding requirements, and they want new teachers to share their understandings. However, they find themselves engaged in coding and developing Individual Program Plans (IPPs), which then contributes to the objectification of youth. As Richard, a youth worker, indicated: "[The] problem with the IPPS [is] where a lot of suggestions being made [by new teachers] are contrary to the way things are done here. So we're constantly struggling with this language, well it's more than a language problem...I tend to see the language of these suggestions as sort of referring to the student as almost an 'it.' And I think that we've tried hard to treat them as an 'I'—somebody who's to be valued."

The coding requirements, however, are *making* teachers see students as "its." How do you value what someone is saying while simultaneously noting the number of times they swear? Senior teachers and youth workers are caught up in the contradictions that are inherent in a coding process that constructs students as deviant. Students are constructed in terms of their special needs through a process that makes it difficult for teachers and youth workers to then reconstruct them as active subjects, as people with feelings, opinions, and needs.

The challenge is to reconcile the need for funding with the need to understand youth. As one teacher noted, "They're intelligent people who as youth survived by their wit." Those survival skills are now being coded as pathological. James told me, "In this inner-city environment getting 90s in high school doesn't bring you a lot of status. Being tough does, though, having drugs in your pocket does, being able to steal a car if you want to, those kinds of things bring you status....But it's also getting away with things, whatever it is. Manipulating and moving around. They're the things that bring success in this environment. But when you get to school you can't use those skills at all."

The requirements of coding certainly indicate agreement with the unacceptability of these skills in schools. But James reflected a different understanding. "Everything has changed [when you get to school] and you've got to start over, so then you're faced with becoming very humble and doing what you need to do to learn and forgetting everything else that you've had to do to succeed. And also the friends that you've developed and habits that you have and that's quite a challenge...it doesn't happen in two weeks for sure...there's a whole new value system that has to come into play."

Given this understanding of youth, the zero tolerance approach underlying the rationale of the coding process seems a bit harsh. It also seems to feed the beliefs that new teachers coming to WRS bring with them. As Kristine, said, "Teachers don't know how to respond to the students and they respond in ways often that are not helpful...I mean teachers are trained to be in charge."

We need to find ways for this special schooling model and coding to inform one another. We also need to incorporate what we, as teachers, *know* about youth into the coding process. We need to take into account the literacies mentioned above that aren't listed on the referral for intake and IPP progress report lists. In a critical pedagogy classroom we can also teach this seeming contradiction, acknowledging the ways youths' thoughts, feelings, and beliefs have been informed by schools and the street.

While we try to protect students from the realities of coding, they know it is being done. I think that talking with students about the ways they are constructed through coding could lead both teachers and students to a critical awareness of the street skills needed for survival and school skills needed for academic success. We could find a balance in that discussion somehow. Such conversations could help students understand and work through the transition from the street to the school.

CONFORMING, CONFRONTING, CO-CREATING

THE FRAMEWORK, THEN, in a nutshell and however messy, follows:

At WRS, learning opportunities are equal to creating the conditions that are necessary for a critical pedagogy. Content is not king here! Before teachers can engage in critical dialogue with students they, along with youth workers, must attend to the more immediate needs of students. The school's program is designed to be flexible in order to meet these student needs while also meeting the needs of the Alberta curriculum. Early service teachers struggle to find a balance between being flexible enough while conforming to the constraints of government structures that define such aspects of schooling as student finance requirements. This balance is in constant flux. Learning to live with this uncertainty as a teacher is complicated by the need to also examine one's own values about classroom practice and the choices being made about curricular content taught.

In order to teach at WRS, one must understand the ways in which poverty, and associated adverse living conditions and early socialization of students, has created psychological pressures for the youth. The students' life experiences are fraught with difficulty in schools, with social services, and the justice system. In addition, teachers must understand that culture, race, gender, sexual orientation, and geographic location all inform these youth and, as such, must inform considerations for teaching.

Other struggles at WRS involve values that seem to be at odds. Teachers often feel that they need to reshape youths' values to be more conducive to academic success in schools. At the same time, teachers must help students to build confidence, and to do so they need to value, to a certain extent, the students' street knowledge. But the attitudes and behaviours needed for school success are in opposition with the knowledge valued on the street. Another tension apparent during discussions in the classroom relates to questions of inclusion and acceptance. Whose knowledge is being taught and valued in schools? Again, teachers must dig deeper and become familiar with other ways of knowing; they must choose to understand their students. When this happens, teachers become critical of their own values, and they interrogate the reasons for the youth's behaviours within the school context: they begin to look at their relationships with urban youth anew.

Teachers at WRS take up critical practices in a variety of ways. Much of my engagement with the ideas of critical pedagogy at the school comes from my own teaching there, as well as academic study. Learning to construct a critical practice requires attentive reflection and a willingness to stumble through blunders (which is not comfortable). To take up a critical practice at wrs is to deny everything you are taught about "managing" a classroom. However, when you are comfortable with this consistently challenging process, you find it is a necessary component of relationships of mutual trust. Staff members at wrs know the importance of building respectful relationships with students. Youth feel that teachers and youth workers value and care about them.

At wrs, students and staff practice critical questioning through the arts and literacy programs. Writing, reading, video, digital media, and photography provide a framework for viewing the community and experiences of youth within it. These media offer opportunities for opening up conversations and create teachable moments within relevant themes. The artistic process, and the conversations surrounding it, also encourages us as educators to examine our own assumptions about the inner city of our community. wrs grew out of a popular theatre process whereby disenfranchised urban youth began to explore their own social realities, formulate understandings, and work toward solving their personal problems. This practice continues to be an important component of the school. Youth in the school point to the ways in which important insights can be developed through the popular theatre process. These same youth advocate the importance of integrated schooling programs as a necessary component of learning to live together.

Funding requirements of a school that addresses the needs of disenfranchised, early school leavers are substantial and require a great deal of time and energy to access. At times these funding concerns impede the abilities of staff to pursue pedagogical practices that are in keeping with student needs. However, financial considerations are a daily reality of alternative educational programs that operate in the inner city and outside the public system. At present, the school receives substantial funding to support special needs students in the school. While this funding ensures wrs's continued existence, it creates difficulties, as well. The process of coding required in order to access these funds depends on a vision of the youth's behaviours as pathological. The resulting objectification of youth prevents new teachers, particularly, from seeing these students as active subjects, "real people," a necessity if one is to engage in critical dialogue.

THE FOLLOWING CHAPTER considers the majority of students at WRS who are Aboriginal. Teachers and youth workers must understand specific learning needs and what conditions might need to be created in order for pedagogy to be effective with Aboriginal students. Is poverty experienced differently in a culture that has been consistently devalued by Canadian society? When we work to re-shape values and build confidence in schools, must these values consider cultural background? How do Aboriginal ways of knowing inform what is taught in schools? These issues are engaged and made complex by the voices at WRS.

TWO COMFORT THAT ELUDES:
FOR DISENFRANCHISED URBAN ABORIGINAL YOUTH

Until you understand that your own culture dictates how you translate everything you see and hear, you will never be able to see or hear things in any other way.[1]

When you look at how cooperative units and collectives, which had to survive over thousands of generations, developed their societal systems and cultures, then philosophies, theories, and cosmologies related to how difference must be celebrated and embraced begin to emerge. You begin to see how difference is perceived, not as race, but as something valuable, something that is strengthening, and something that is absolutely necessary.[2]

THERE IS A GREAT DEBATE about what educational practices are best suited to meet the needs of Aboriginal youth, both on and off reserves. Some support separate programs with cultural underpinnings, others push for integration in public schools. I have found that WRS—a school that has been designed to serve disenfranchised urban youth, no matter what their cultural background—meets the needs of Aboriginal students, who make up the majority of the school's student population. Not having a voice in public schools or seeing themselves reflected in the curriculum often leads to Aboriginal youth leaving public schools for separate programs built on values and beliefs that Aboriginal students have in common, and which give the youth voice and opportunities.

In Alberta, segregated programs for specific groups of learners include black, Aboriginal, and religious youth. We see alternative schools as a tool for protecting minority rights. As well, urban schools developed with considerable Aboriginal control and focused on cultural survival have emerged across Canada. The Wandering Spirit School in Toronto, Plains Indian Survival School in Calgary, and Joe Duquette High School in Saskatoon are a few examples. Certainly the issue of segregated versus integrated schools for Aboriginal learners is more complex than an either-or model would illuminate. The growing body of critical scholarship focused on redefining beliefs, communities, and spirituality in relation to schooling for Aboriginal students reflects just how complex the issue has become.

The arguments in favour of schools specifically designed for Aboriginal students are indeed valid, however, WRS offers an alternative understanding of the ways in which disenfranchised youth may wish to be, and arguably can be, successfully included in integrated school programs. Here, people can live their lives together and share a subculture with common life experiences beyond racial lines. At the same time, within the WRS classroom, tensions do emerge in discussions with youth regarding both their experiences of segregation and integration. These tensions lead teachers and students to questions about comfort. The youth I spoke to as I conducted my study of WRS had not been at all comfortable in any of the schools they had attended prior to WRS. I sought to discover why this was, and what WRS was doing to make these students feel comfortable.

THE LIMITATIONS OF EXPERIENCE

THROUGH WORKING AT a school for disenfranchised urban youth I have developed a desire to understand how best to educate Aboriginal students in my classroom. I have searched through literature and mined conversations for common observations about successes that I might be able to apply in my own classroom, to guide my own practice. Certainly there is no shortage of opinions on ways education should and should not unfold for Aboriginal students. But all of those opinions become difficult to reconcile. How could I best educate Aboriginal youth when there was no agreement on method in either existing practices or written accounts? I came to the conclusion that I needed to look beyond the opinions of others and develop my own approaches based on my relations within the school in which I worked.

I used to have ideas about what "typical" and "regular" behaviour of Aboriginal students were, based on previous experiences with Aboriginal people. These perceptions were, of course, general, and I thus, at first, failed to acknowledge the individual differences and unique lived experiences of my students. The assumptions underlying my practice denied them the opportunity to speak for themselves about who they were and wanted to be. I began to understand that seeing individuals as a "means" toward understanding a universal meant that I was missing out on understanding individuals as "ends" in themselves. Individuals have value simply as individuals. Each experience with an individual has the potential to speak to us, if we are open to the experience.

In the past, I entered into relationships with Aboriginal scholars with certain expectations. In particular, I expected to be treated badly because I am white. After all, haven't white people treated Aboriginal people badly in the past (and *still*, some would argue)? I expected resentment for those past wrongs. Unfortunately, by entering into conversations with these preconceived notions, I ended up looking for generalities, a means to confirm earlier experiences. I was looking for what was predictable.

In my dealings with Aboriginal peoples, I tried to understand how the past has shaped the present and be understanding of anger even when directed at me. I tried to understand my counterpart's point of view through ongoing reflection. There was a constant struggle for mutual recognition, which resulted in tension and sometimes the domination of one person over the other. As I looked for regularities in behaviour to inform my teaching and writing, my attempts at "genuine" understanding were dangerously close to being attempts at finding the "essence" of Aboriginality. As if there is such a thing. Any claim to understanding another person in advance serves the purpose of keeping that person's thoughts, feelings, and beliefs at a distance. Unfortunately, many of our approaches to policy and practice for youth who are disenfranchised make this claim to understanding. For example, in order to claim special needs funding at WRS, we must subject the students to the pre-set requirements of coding. This process, of course, is in direct opposition to the wealth of understandings possible through emancipatory teaching.

How have I become aware of the limitations of my past experience in trying to come to a "genuine" understanding of Aboriginal youth and applying that understanding to my teaching practice? I learn about myself as I pursue relations with Aboriginal scholars and others, people connected through shared values regarding schooling and goals related to inclusion of those who have been disenfranchised. In particular, one of my colleagues was initially excited about engaging in a project at WRS but then decided the school didn't have what she was looking for: a program with a foundation of Aboriginal culture and taught by Aboriginal teachers. For my part, I had come to believe that the program at WRS was working well for disenfranchised urban Aboriginal students. I called my own belief about WRS and education for Aboriginal youth into question at this point, and I realized that I needed to discuss my perspective with others. When I spoke with James about this, he told me how the program seems to promote positive self-images for young people. Following is a snippet of our conversation:

> Diane: I think there is a [societal] change in the way Aboriginal youth feel about themselves.
> James: It's fostered here...I think that people with Native background feel better about it here than they would maybe somewhere else [public schools].
> Diane: Any thoughts on how it is fostered here?
> James: General acceptance of who you are.

Although I acknowledge the potential value of programs designed specifically around Aboriginal culture, such as Amiskwaciy (an Edmonton public school for Aboriginal students), I do believe that other alternatives, like WRS, also have something to offer.

While there are good reasons to argue that there is something fundamentally different about Aboriginal worldviews stemming from spiritual and traditional cultures, a staunch promotion of the "Aboriginal worldview" as something concrete risks enforcing categorical differences based on cultural generalizations. In addition, I believe that promoting separate programs for Aboriginal youth ignores the need for mainstream schools to improve their responsiveness to Aboriginal students and to foster greater understanding among non-Aboriginal students. When my colleague rejected WRS as a site for an Aboriginal education project, I gained these insights. Then, I moved forward with greater confidence, feeling I could find the possibilities for contact and understanding that were constantly emerging in my classroom and through my research.

The tension highlighted here, of segregation versus integration in schools, is apparent in the experiences of disenfranchised urban youth, as well. When we are conscious of our shared history and the traditions of schooling in Canada, we are awakened to other experiences. Consciousness opens up possibilities for understanding not only ourselves but also disenfranchised urban youth. These possibilities, I have found, however, are not always easy to explore. We need to place ourselves in the experiences of others while simultaneously understanding our own lived reality. Without exploring this tension, we remain committed to our own beliefs and deny the possibility of other ideas.

THE TENSIONS OF TOGETHERNESS

THERE ARE CERTAIN TENSIONS that come from the close togetherness students and teachers experience in school settings, and the tensions are even greater at schools like WRS, where all discussions and actions are prefaced by the experiences of urban youth. Teachers and youth workers also come together prefaced by their experiences, some closely related to the youth's experiences and some not so related. The following conversation exemplifies the struggle between tensions of segregation and integration, of how to promote group cohesion while affirming individual identities.

When I spoke to Leonard, an Aboriginal youth worker at WRS, I started dismantling the ideas I previously had about the value of a certain program for Aboriginal students. Leonard, a graduate of WRS, entered and attended the University of Alberta and the Transition Year Program (TYP). The TYP is designed to provide access to university programs for Aboriginal students who may not qualify for direct entry into a specific faculty.

Leonard: When I was in the TYP program, I didn't complete for one... which was no fault but my own. Um, I felt completely uncomfortable when I was there. It almost seemed like they were promoting racism and separatism.

Diane: The TYP program?

Leonard: Yeah.

Diane: So if you were in a regular education program you probably would have been...

Leonard: I probably would have been happier. I would have wanted to go to class.

Diane: Yeah.

Leonard: I used to get picked on in class. They used to call me a red apple and stuff like that.

Diane: Oh, why?

Leonard: And these were my peers. Because I, what was it one of the girls called me...a white sympathizer. Well, I'm half white.

Diane: Yeah.

Leonard: I just felt completely uncomfortable and I made a few complaints and said, "Look, I don't feel comfortable writing about this particular subject," and if you don't write on that subject then you fail and you don't get marked for it.

Diane: Was it a subject about Native students or Native people?

Leonard: It was how the white man...how do you feel your life has been affected by the white man stealing your language? I didn't feel comfortable writing on that because...

Diane: You have to agree that they stole your language?

Leonard: Exactly. Well, I have to agree, but at the same point in time it wasn't mine to begin with. I wasn't raised like that. Like I'm...my mother's white.

This conversation with Leonard opened my eyes. How do we engage with historical issues in schools without having students feel they are betraying themselves, their friends, or their family members, and without assuming a coherent unitary student identity? Leonard's comments raise questions about how we promote group cohesion and affirm individual identities while simultaneously promoting cross-cultural understandings. Sara, a WRS student, reflected on this very same dilemma:

> *People need something to identify with...they could learn something they didn't know about their heritage, but I don't think it should be focused on one culture. I think it should be a mix of things...and maybe you adapt that to your life so that it goes around and creates less racism.*

These tensions are a part of life, of course, but, at school, we need to work through the tension together if we are to learn anything from it.

DECONSTRUCTING "REGULAR"

PART OF WORKING OUT tensions involves asking questions. Only when you ask directed questions can you glean knowledge that is gained from experience. What knowledge did I gain from my conversation with Leonard? I wondered: *do* segregated educational programs, designed for specific cultural groups, promote racism? I think I wanted to believe the answer was yes. Such an idea fit with my belief that integrated programs are necessary if we are to learn to live together. When Leonard said, "I felt completely uncomfortable," I thought, "Shouldn't this type of program have made him feel more comfortable?" As he said, "these were my peers." At the same time, for some students, the TYP *is* a comfortable setting. One participant in the program commented, "It's kind

49

of a family-oriented atmosphere."[3] So why did Leonard feel uncomfortable? What might have been different for him? While issues of race and the fact that this youth has one Aboriginal parent and one white parent need to be explored, it seems to me that the ways in which he was shaped by his former street life may have been a contributing factor in his lack of comfort in the TYP.

In order to understand the experiences of students in the TYP and other programs for Aboriginal youth, one must take socioeconomic and class differences into account. The mainstream educator's belief about what is a "regular" program and what isn't can also contribute to disenfranchised student discomfort. Why might some students feel their involvement in segregated programs, designed to validate identities and provide safe comfort zones, leave them feeling confused and uncomfortable? Other students respond well to these segregated settings. I began to think that it would be important to question the notion of "regular" and deconstruct terms like "red apple." I hoped it would help disenfranchised urban youth to be able to become more comfortable if they could be critical of the words and ideas that seemed to be pinning them down. A critical student body paired with an educator who understood how youth are shaped by the street would help schools meet student needs in any educational setting.

CONSCIOUSNESS-RAISING EDUCATION

LITTLE CLASSROOM RESEARCH has been done on the effects of teaching students about their culture, history, and languages. It is generally considered that teaching these elements yields positive educational results. Similarly, content about oppression, racism, and differences in worldviews is felt to be beneficial. Consciousness-raising courses at all levels of formal education have encouraged new hopes amongst disenfranchised students generally and have raised the educational aspirations of Aboriginal students. We have also seen growth in educational attainment within the Aboriginal population, but with little classroom research to back up this statement, we don't know for certain what types of educational successes may be attributed to the inclusion of cultural content and discussions of power differentials in classrooms. Still, it seems difficult to dispute the idea that new hopes and dreams have sprung from understanding that poverty and oppression are not the result of personal shortcomings but rather are the result of a culture that has traditionally been devalued in Canada.

Consciousness-raising courses can also impart the knowledge that poverty and oppression have been tools created by institutions in order to maintain the status quo and to foster and legitimize social divisions. Finding out about this can lead some students to feel uncomfortable with how they are positioned within society; witness my conversation with Leonard above. If this is the case, is it only mixed-race students who might feel uncomfortable, or might other Aboriginal students also feel disjointed? It makes me wonder how educators might work with this discomfort as a starting point for dialogue, and try to find out who is in the best place to work with this discomfort. In mainstream schools, those positioned to create dialogue hold power and privilege over those who are disenfranchised. As educators we need to find out how to allow space for Aboriginal consciousness and identity to thrive without adhering to generalized notions of what non-Aboriginal people think versus what Aboriginal people think. We need to find out what is comfortable so that the disenfranchised students can be encouraged to reach their hopes and dreams.

I followed up my conversation with Leonard with another conversation. This time another former student and Aboriginal youth worker, Claire, joined us.

Claire: I was just thinking that...I think it was maybe you, Leonard, who said that it might promote racism going into an Aboriginal-based course, or something like that, just because they're Aboriginal.
Diane: Mmmhmm.
Claire: I could see that point of view because, I mean, in the real world we don't have that, the work place [isn't] set up for just you know, Leonard just works for Native people.
Diane: Yeah.

51

Leonard and Claire seemed to be saying they would be more comfortable in integrated programs. However, comfort in these settings is also unlikely, based on their prior experiences in public schools. And, in terms of university classes, I don't imagine Leonard would have been comfortable in a mixed program, either. He could have avoided discussing painful topics, but he may still have felt like a fish out of water—both Aboriginal and poor in an environment that is largely white and middle class. As James explained, "There's a whole different syntax involved in the way of presenting yourself. And not only that, it's the stepping out of your environment, which is about as uncomfortable for a young person as it would be for you [Diane] to start living in the inner-city environment on a daily basis. Your language would be as out of place in the inner city as theirs is when they come into the [middle-] class environment at the university."

Staff members at WRS seemed to be saying that youth need to develop dominant middle-class ways to survive in mainstream society. This is an important consideration when preparing youth to enter post-secondary studies, but I think the youth were saying they *should* be comfortable in integrated public-school settings. They should be accepted for who they are. Leonard and Claire were expressing an ideal, a world that doesn't (yet) exist.

The point of many segregated programs is that these students *don't* feel comfortable in integrated settings. In order for segregated programs for Aboriginal students to exist, concrete opposition from mainstream society is essential. Without such institutions and their impact on Aboriginal people, there would be no need for segregated educational programs. This tension reflects the opposing nature of these two types of institutions. They oppose each other, and yet, without one there would be no need for the other. They are interconnected. In order to engage with this tension at school, we need to recognize the inherent *value* in the tension, that struggle is vital to growth. We need to engage with such struggles in schools—both in segregated and integrated settings.

Let's look at the term "red apple." The image of a red apple seems to epitomize the contradiction of living in two interconnected worlds.

The ways in which we reconcile the contradictions in our lives are influenced and regulated by societal norms. Terms such as "red apple" are used to convey displeasure with the ways in which these tensions are engaged.

In the following conversation, Leonard and Claire get at this need to engage with issues, but not only with other Aboriginal people. Rather, it seems to be important that we engage with *all* parties implicated in these issues.

> *Claire: It would be the same if we kept our kids at home and taught* 53
> *them at home schooling.*
> *Diane: Yeah.*
> *Claire: Then they don't get that social aspect and then they don't know*
> *how to interact with other kids.*
> *Diane: Yeah.*
> *Claire: And it's the same if it were to be just Aboriginal and white.*
> *Leonard: A child needs to develop those social skills at an early age or*
> *else, you know, they'll be sitting up on a bell tower when they're older*
> *and...*
> *Diane: Yeah...okay. So then does the same hold true of a program like*
> *[school for Aboriginal youth]?*
> *Leonard: From the youth who have gone through our program who*
> *have gone through [school for Aboriginal youth] I've heard nothing*
> *but bad things....From everyone that I've spoken with, they've said the*
> *same thing that, it was almost, there was too much racism. It was all*
> *about white bashing.*

The struggles inherent in the conversation I had with Leonard and Claire need to be engaged with in schools.

Leonard and Claire weren't comfortable with experiences with programs designed to develop Aboriginal consciousness. Why did they end up feeling this way? What led them to a conclusion that racism dominated a program designed to develop an awareness of systems of oppression under which they themselves have suffered? Certainly other Aboriginal students find these programs affirm their identities through validation of cultural values and a greater sense of belonging. Leonard and Claire, however, didn't experience that same sense of belonging in these programs. Yet they experienced racism and exclusion in public-school settings, as well.

While these youth say that Aboriginal students need to be together with non-Aboriginal students to engage in struggles, certainly others believe they can be engaged more effectively from within the parameters of a segregated program. Togetherness may be laden with tension, but there are benefits of articulating conflicts and working through them. Certainly the possibility of engaging with struggles exists in both segregated and integrated programs.

Leonard and Claire's experiences of disenfranchisement may have led them to express sentiments about multiculturalism, as noted in the following conversation, yet what they said suggests we need to engage further in discussions of these issues.

Leonard: I don't want to put my own foot in my mouth here but people are still fuming over what happened a hundred, two hundred years ago.
Diane: Mmmhmm.
Leonard: And by putting programs, separate programs for individual cultures and groups, that's just adding fuel to the fire. That's just feeding it.
Diane: Feeds it?
Leonard: And Canada's supposed to be about multiculturalism.
Diane: Yeah.
Leonard: You know and that's how I was raised and that's what I believe is that we should all be together.
Diane: Yeah. Well, the argument is that maybe those things happened a hundred years ago but the racism continues today. So...if you felt you were abused growing up because of your skin colour or whatever?
Leonard: I was. It happened to me. You know, I suffered racism several times.
Claire: Even I did. I mean I don't look Native at all...but my family does, my mom definitely does.
Diane: Mmmhmm.

Claire: And when we lived in [name of city]...it's a city but it's very small...and our family was one of, you know, the 5 per cent in the whole city that was Native, and it was obvious, and, ah, I never felt so much of it. I guess my sister and brother did a bit.

Diane: Mmmhmm, do they look more Native, your sister and brother?

Claire: Yeah.

Leonard: Especially her brother.

Diane: The community I grew up in, a little town in rural Manitoba, the Native kids had a really, really difficult time. There's two things... they're also poor...

55

Claire: Exactly.

Diane: And so, you know the middle-class people don't talk to the poor people and the white people don't talk to the Native people. So if you're Native and poor, forget it.

Leonard: Yes, sir.

Diane: You're down there living by the river and nobody's talking to you ever.

Claire: Yeah, we were on welfare, too. My mom was alone.

Diane: Yeah, so that adds to the whole and it's hard to separate what's causing what...

But simply putting everyone together isn't going to get at the issues that were raised in this dialogue. For example, contrary to the above comment that "Canada is supposed to be about multiculturalism," Aboriginal people have special status in Canada, distinct from official multiculturalism. A focus on multiculturalism may reflect Leonard's lack of awareness or it may indicate that he would be more comfortable without special status. Being like everybody else attracts less attention. It's certainly a way to avoid talking about issues that are uncomfortable, to avoid addressing our past.

Leonard and Claire have suggested being separated into racial groups may feed racist tendencies, leading me to question whether integrated programs could work at interrogating the issues through critical dialogue. In both segregated and integrated programs, we need to face issues through critical discussions, even though the process of doing so is often not comfortable. It appears that comfort eludes Aboriginal students in both segregated and integrated settings. Working through issues together, with a consideration of who holds power in the discussions, may lead all of us to a place of greater comfort when we come to understand our shared history and lived experiences. For me, the question isn't so much about segregated versus integrated schools but rather about comfort for disenfranchised youth. It's about creating spaces where youth can have a voice, be validated in their personal lives and experiences, and find comfort through acceptance. And, maybe it's about approaches that question the issues in ways that allow people to respect themselves *and* others.

FEELING UNCOMFORTABLE IN SCHOOLS

THERE ARE SO MANY questions we must ask ourselves when we consider how to make urban Aboriginal youth feel at home in school. How can educators foster a sense of belonging in former students and current ones? Is belonging a physical place or a social space? Why have they felt uncomfortable in the past? Historically, since the arrival of Western forms of education, schooling has been fraught with difficulties for Aboriginal families. In Canada, the government forced assimilation on Aboriginal families via the residential school system. Well-documented accounts of residential school experiences clearly point to environments where Aboriginal students did not feel comfortable in the least. These schools were founded and operated on the belief that separating children from their family and communities would be the best way to assimilate them into "normal" Canadian society. Verbal and physical abuse was a regular occurrence. These school environments, obviously, were more than uncomfortable. Today, Aboriginal youth continue to live with the legacy of residential schools—in communities and families that were spiritually, emotionally, and physically damaged by the school system they were forced to be a part of. Disenfranchised urban Aboriginal students still struggle for a "fit" in schools. They still are looking for a place to belong.

Questions heap upon questions when we consider factors other than cultural heritage in disenfranchised students' lives. What about those students who are also poor? Those whose mothers are raising them alone, without support, on social assistance? How about youth who don't have a home, who are fending for themselves on the streets of inner-city Edmonton? These added layers of social difficulty increase the level of discomfort students feel in school. Statistics tell us that Aboriginal youth are disproportionately represented within the population of urban, single parents living in poverty. Canada's Aboriginal population has a high proportion of children and youth. In Alberta approximately half of Aboriginal people live in urban centres.[4] A lower proportion of urban Aboriginal youth live with their parents compared to all other urban youth and a higher proportion live with a partner or as a single parent.

57

I truly believe that another study is needed to consider *degrees* of discomfort and belonging in schools—but I have to pause when I think about what topics such a study should pinpoint. Poverty, gender, whether or not the youth in question are parents, whether or not their parents were single parents—the list of considerations in such a study would be a long one, with each individual item correlating to the others in many and varied ways. Considering the relationship between gender, Aboriginality, and discomfort in schools, for example, we can see from my dialogue with Leonard and Claire that Claire feels her brother and sister experienced more racism than she did because they looked "more Native," not necessarily because of gender. At the same time, single mothers raising children in poverty can be called a gender issue.

What is broken open by Claire's phrase "I don't look Native at all"? What does this mean? When she spoke those words, I had a particular understanding of her meaning based on my previous experiences. I expected her to have been treated badly in her community based on what I knew of her family circumstances and the historical conditions of urban Aboriginal people living in Canada. It fit with what I *knew* to be the experiences of Aboriginal people in the community in which I grew up. My community was racist. It ignored poor people. None of us talked to poor, Aboriginal people, not even in our own classrooms. I had one Aboriginal friend as a child, and she had been adopted into a white family. They weren't wealthy, but they weren't poor either. They went to our church. My family approved of them. I often think of my former Aboriginal classmates, many of whom are now dead. I know we contributed to their deaths, by ignoring them. I know that the community contributed to those deaths by not giving their parents jobs. Power in the community and school was held by those who were white and middle class. I know those students didn't finish school because they couldn't stand to be there. They weren't comfortable in that school in Manitoba in the 1960s and 1970s just as Aboriginal youth aren't comfortable in schools here and now.

Achieving comfort, though, means achieving respect and acceptance. Schools must challenge existing relations and complacent acceptance of the status quo. We have to work through discomfort to a place of positive change. This, of course, means upsetting the balance. We all have to enter into a place where we all will feel uncomfortable, but we have to do this to reach the goal: more positive relations in schools.

My conversations with Leonard and Claire helped me to think about new directions for emancipatory discussion in schools. Does "looking Native" imply that a person might not want to? It seems that a person would experience less racism that way. Residential schools were prime sites for developing cultural self-hatred along with ongoing societal attitudes of mainstream dominance. I understand how these feelings of shame, projected by dominant social structures, might exist. In our conversation, Leonard also said, "growing up as a kid myself, I never used to tell people I was Native. I used to tell people I was Italian." This made me think about how mixed-race people in mainstream society have traditionally had negative experiences because dominant society doesn't know how to "classify" them. More recently, society has come to celebrate "hybridity," and people of mixed cultural backgrounds may choose to occupy spaces at both the centre and the margins. However, Leonard, in claiming a completely different heritage, was doing something different. He has one Aboriginal parent and one white parent. No Italian ancestry anywhere. So instead of moving between and across categories in a comfortable fashion, he was looking to pass himself off as something different from what he actually is. He wasn't comfortable with himself. Or more accurately, he had been made to feel uncomfortable about himself by those who hadn't accepted him.

I certainly didn't *expect* him or others to be comfortable. I have met Aboriginal people in recent years who *are* comfortable and caused me to rethink earlier expectations I had held. These are people who demonstrate pride in a rich cultural tradition and who engage in both traditional and contemporary cultural practices. They are also people who either felt accepted in their early school years or who have come to find acceptance in more recent experiences. Their behaviours, their speech, the way they move through the world shows, like Leonard came to believe, "our culture is beautiful." All of these people experienced a sense of community within their schools and were transformed by an exploration of culture.

I reject the notion that things or people are naturally a certain way. I know that experiences I had growing up were not reflective of all experiences. But why are some Aboriginal people more comfortable than others? I have found that Aboriginal people who are also poor have significant problems with discomfort in schools and society in general. The most uncomfortable of the Aboriginal poor are those who suffer from poverty that results from particular historical relations in Canada that devalued Aboriginal culture. Location is a factor, as well. Inner cities are more fragmented and less conducive to finding and sharing common cultural values. There are problems of pervasive poverty on many reserves in Canada, as well, yet Edmonton's inner city has its own unique brand of paucity. Economically and socially isolated from the rest of the city, we can sometimes find it easy to ignore what is lacking. The day-to-day struggles to survive here are made increasingly difficult by a harsh climate and a political environment that isn't conducive to helping the poor. In order to confront the problem, we need to consider how families and communities have been fragmented, how many youth are floating without anchors.

Leonard felt that he started feeling more at home in school when he began to believe that Aboriginal cultures are beautiful. We talked about social class, as well.

Leonard: I know several people who mock me because I live in this area and they say, "Oh, every time I drive through I roll up my windows and lock the doors." Why? What for? Because you know there's a guy

drinking on the bench? You know there's more crime happens out in [name of city] and [name of community in Edmonton] than actually happens down here.
Diane: Mmmhmm.
Leonard: At least down here I wouldn't have to worry about shootings.
Diane: Right.
Leonard: I have to worry about people asking me for spare change or cigarettes. You know that's the harshest thing that I've experienced around here.

Clearly he's comfortable with his inner-city neighbourhood. In contrast, my neighbourhood is predominantly middle class and predominantly white. Leonard talked about crime and the perception that there is more of it in the inner city. I believed that at first, too. It was uncomfortable wandering around the inner city. In part, I didn't belong and it appeared to me that people I met on the street shared that opinion. Was it me or was it them? If I *looked* uncomfortable then it would appear that I didn't belong. Do socioeconomic differences need to be such a barrier? Easy for me to say; I have more than I need. But I think Leonard made an important point about perceptions. In the end, maybe we all need to feel comfortable somewhere, but not necessarily in the same place. The notion that my neighbourhood is one to aspire to is ethnocentric. But it isn't ethnocentric to assume all people need to have a safe place, both physically and psychologically, where basic needs are met. This is yet another tension-filled topic that begs to be addressed in schools.

BECOMING COMFORTABLE IN SCHOOLS

How do we disrupt the current social order so that all students can feel more comfortable in schools? Where "regular" means all students and all schools? A place where all young people experience a sense of belonging? Teachers using a critical pedagogy can work toward such possibilities: by thinking critically, questioning, and encouraging students to think critically, we can begin to move toward a goal of respect and acceptance. We can engage all students' life experiences, not just those of people currently occupying positions of cultural dominance. Thinking about the word "comfortable" leads me to thoughts of well-being, ease, and satisfaction. The thesaurus offers "peaceful" as a synonym. Similarly, the word "uncomfortable" offers alternatives such as "self-consciousness" and "embarrassment." How do we move from being embarrassed to feeling at peace? The word embarrassment takes me back to my discussion with Leonard. In reference to youth at WRS, he said, "They come to believe the stereotype, then it gets to the point where they, some of them, have felt it's embarrassing to be Native." Leonard, however, has made this transition from being embarrassed (telling others he is Italian) to feeling at peace (our culture is beautiful). We can learn from an examination of his experiences.

I decided to follow up on my discussion with Leonard and Claire and talk about how to help others move into a peaceful space. They spoke of both traditional and contemporary cultural practices and about providing youth with information and resources that they could choose to access when and if they are ready.

> Diane: I wonder if it is something you come to as you get older...
> if maybe you start wanting to know more about it [one's family and cultural traditions].
> Leonard: When I was younger I was embarrassed. I was embarrassed to be Native and I didn't care. I didn't want to know anything about my culture. I was actually embarrassed because I knew how to smudge during a sweet grass ceremony.
> Diane: Mmmhmm.
> Leonard: Like I was, that was embarrassing to me because all my friends would look at me like, "Oh, good God, man, what are you, how do you know how to do that," and I was embarrassed of it but as I got older I wanted to know more and more. I think it helped shape me and who I am.

As we continued our conversation, we moved into talking about contemporary cultural practices. Claire commented on a particular student: "Last year...I took part in a workshop...one of the kids from [a school for disenfranchised urban youth]...he was very much into the hip hop culture and Native culture and he could talk about it for hours, you know if you just asked one question he'd go on and on and on...I mean he was obviously proud of it."

Through our conversation, I realized that there could be many ways of identifying with and being proud of one's cultural heritage. One youth was comfortable with more traditional forms of cultural practice and the other through more contemporary modes of expression. So what led to their comfort? It seems it was not so much the form of expression but rather how it made them feel. Proud. Comfortable? Peaceful? Both of these youth attended schools that were not focused on cultural practices but rather on particular pedagogies for disenfranchised youth. So how did they come to pursue their cultural roots? Leonard and Claire suggest it is in an environment where people feel respected, and where the information is available, that young people might just choose a form of expression that reflects and validates who they feel they are. Mayan educator Agustin Sapon Morales agrees with this sentiment in a 2000 interview:

> It is important that we identify ourselves as Indian people. So, we shouldn't be ashamed of our languages, of our dress, of our customs— there are many things—and we shouldn't be ashamed of them. Unfortunately, the education that we got in school, they have never taught us any of these things. But respect is real and important to communication.[5]

Certainly Leonard and Claire and all the other students at WRS weren't taught to respect material elements of culture in schools, but they weren't taught respect in general, either, as reflected in these comments by both Aboriginal and non-Aboriginal students, Kevin, Kelsey, Dylan, and Joel:

> When I was in [public] high school, the teachers they're not friendly.

> I had some pretty bad experiences because all the schools I went to, if you weren't like a certain type of person then nobody liked you and you

got picked on...the teachers would just turn the other cheek, whatever, they just didn't care about it.

The teachers judged me on my marks and treated me by their judgments...and they'd be like, "Ok, this kid's like basically a waste of time."

I didn't like the way I was being treated, that's all.

Respect needs to be taught in schools—first and foremost by show-
ing respect for students—and we need to learn about each other and about ourselves. We need to model respect. Morales identifies the Mayan way of doing this: "In the Maya culture, the way we should respect the Elders is obedience. Also, when a child gets up, they have to bow their heads to the Elder, and the grandfather puts his right hand on the child's head. That's the signal of protection."[6] Through this practice children learn respect, but also that they are respected and cared for. Many of the youth in this study pointed to teachers' lack of respect for them as factors in why they felt uncomfortable in school and why they left. As Joel, an Aboriginal student at WRS, said, "They'll [WRS teachers] actually help out when you need it. They won't push you away like normal schools might."

WRS students have also told me the respect they feel from teachers at WRS is an important element in their current school experiences. Dylan, a non-Aboriginal student, reflected on a general feeling he had detected amongst the students at WRS: "Teachers here don't look at you as a student, they look at you as a person and a student so they treat you like both...you can call teachers by their first names here, which is also a sign of respect, too, in a way." Vicky and Joel, two Aboriginal students, added, "I like the way that you could be friends with your teachers...they got more time for you," and "I find it a lot easier here...there's not that much to worry about...like, teachers, they can joke around with you."

These students really felt they had the respect of their teachers at WRS and were comfortable in the "dynamics of the school [that] are...at a perfect temperature," in the words of Ian, another student.

Tensions of togetherness frame the stories that are told in critical conversations at WRS. Understanding that Aboriginal, "mixed-race," and white students all make up the population of disenfranchised urban youth can lead us to an awareness that there is no such thing as a "typical" or "regular" youth experience. As I've discovered, comfort—a sense of belonging—eludes these inner-city youth. And we all must become uncomfortable in critical conversations before we can struggle through to a peaceful place where we can all find ways to learn and live together.

At WRS, a critical pedagogy approach brings all youth to a place of understanding social issues and comfort by including everyone in discussions. While the process may be uncomfortable, inclusion is inherently more comfortable than exclusion. Ultimately, through emotional struggle, we can come to a place of greater comfort together. I've discovered that it is also important for these youth that their comfort is not achieved at the expense of other's comfort. They want to respect themselves *and* others.

WHILE THESE YOUTH may be at home at WRS, I continue to question whether this is comfort derived from avoidance of places where they feel uncomfortable. It seems we need to continue to trouble the notion of "regular" to move to an understanding of all programs and all students as "regular." We need to embrace difference. Leonard and Claire's comments on segregated educational programs suggest that educators need to move away from championing one or the other of the opposing, yet interlinked, separate versus integrated programs; rather, we need to find ways to create comfortable spaces for disenfranchised urban youth in all schools.

CONSTRUCTING
THE **"SELF"**:

OPPOSITION AND ACCEPTANCE
IN **PUBLIC** SCHOOLS

*Some people think I am peculiar. I don't know how to take that, except
that it must be something that sets me apart, makes me different.
Being different means it isn't easy to belong, isn't easy to be accepted,
but it is also a measure of safety.*[1]

THE YOUTH AT WRS SHARE common public schooling experiences in
which their thoughts, beliefs, feelings, desires, and perspectives were
rejected by interlocking systems of oppression. At public school they
were oppressed because of their poverty, race, and gender, and any
combination of those three factors. We all can examine our own experiences by looking at how our gender, our race, and our position in the
class structure affected our acceptance within the school environment.
Early schooling experiences shape our awareness of self because "self"
is constructed relationally. In the public schooling experiences of WRS
youth, lack of social acceptance has had a significant impact on the
ways in which their "selfs" have been constructed.

RACE AND CLASS DISADVANTAGE

I WILL NEVER FORGET the conversation I had with Sara, a student at WRS,
about her experiences in a large urban public school. She described

how teachers and fellow students' behaviours affected her own beliefs about where she belonged in the school, and she gave me pause to think about how acceptance and rejection in schools can affect students.

> *Sara: The cheerleaders and there were the people who did like the video stuff...they have a studio with cameras, like it was crazy, it was really cool but like they have all that kind of stuff and those kinds of people and even in with the teachers they get treated differently than people who are not so involved with that kind of stuff.*
>
> *Diane: Oh, the teachers have priorities then?*
>
> *Sara: Well, with the students they kind of do like a favouritism thing. Because I remember this, I was in the TV program so I was an anchorperson and what they do is they read the schools' announcements or whatever in the morning and at lunchtime or whatever, so I was like the anchorperson and they had TVs in all the classrooms and you'd go on the TV and you'd read the announcements.*
>
> *Diane: Mmmhmm.*
>
> *Sara: And I was part of that for almost the whole year and at the end of the year they did a big kind of end of the year show and showed all the work that people that were involved in that did and I wasn't in any of the pictures or anything like that. And like the people who were had been in the program for longer or who had more of a relationship with other students or the teachers.*
>
> *Diane: Mmmhmm.*
>
> *Sara: They were all in there, but I wasn't.*

Clearly Sara didn't identify with "those kinds of people" who "get treated differently" by teachers, and her experience as an ignored anchorwoman made her feel even more strongly about her suspicion that teachers have favourites. What is it about these "favourites" that makes them, well, favourites? It's not just the activities they are involved in, as Sara's story about her involvement in the TV program suggests. Is it then a certain type of student who gets involved, and the manner in which they become involved? That is, what would a class, gender, and race analysis of the video club and cheer squad reveal? As another student, Kelsey, said, "to go on the cheer team you have to have I think it's five years dance experience" and "the people in [name of school] their cheer team are like maybe a hundred pounds." For the cheer squad, then, the school is looking for experienced dancers, not street kids who haven't had the class advantages of high-level training opportunities. Cultural capital presumes an expenditure of time and learning that is made possible by possession of economic capital.

I wondered if the youth at WRS understood that economic capital can translate into power and involvement in highly skilled activities and if that understanding shaped the ways in which they thought about themselves? Sara certainly didn't reveal this understanding. She was quick to say her exclusion was because she "was a new student." Yet she also knew she was different from "those kinds of people." It is in such situations that people learn about differences. She understood that she was different whether or not she framed her story about her difference as a class, gender, or race difference. She knew that "people who are not so much into the arts, they don't get as much attention as those who are." And she knew she was different than them. Recognizing her social location in the TV program, Sara had already begun to develop an understanding of herself that was mediated by activities she had participated in and people she had met within those activities.

In discussion about people who are not so much into the arts, who don't get as much attention, Sara went on to say that is "not really fair because there's a lot of people have to go there [to that school] because they're in the neighbourhood." By saying this, she showed that she had an understanding of social class. The neighbourhood she was talking about is a poor one at the core of the inner city. Some youth have to go to that school because they live in the neighbourhood. Others choose to attend from other parts of the city in order to access specialized programming. She knew that it was the neighbourhood youth who were being ignored. At the same time, she took responsibility for her own lack of acceptance. "I was interested in the arts but I'm also very shy so it was [difficult] to be part of those groups." In this way, Sara was allowing herself to save face even as she was developing a defense against oppression.

Identifying herself as shy prevented Sara from acknowledging that the neighbourhood youth, of which she was one, were poor and predominantly Aboriginal or mixed race. Yet acceptance was important, and she hoped to find it.

> *Sara: I had a really hard time trying to make friends. I made a couple of acquaintances that I had lunch with...but that was about it. So I was really lonely...I thought maybe, like you know, in a big school, like that they could have some kind of group or something of new students that have come from other places that didn't know anybody... if you've moved around a lot like I did, you don't have that close group of friends.*
>
> *Diane: Mmmhmm.*
>
> *Sara: So it's a little bit harder. And I found it really difficult in that huge population to make friends.*
>
> *Diane: Yeah.*
>
> *Sara: My whole grade twelve year was really, really difficult, and I think that's part of the reason that I dropped out. Just because I didn't really have any support from people my age...really the only support I had when I went there I was seeing one of those guidance counselors like every other day or something because I was having some difficult times at home, too. But I didn't have any friends for grade twelve, like, nobody. I was totally by myself so it was really, like, actually really depressing.*

In this conversation, Sara was considering her situation relative to others. She could see that others had friends, others had supportive families—others "belonged." She came to the conclusion that in order to find a place to belong she had to become someone else.

> *Sara: There was a lot of people who were really involved in that kind of life [heavily involved in drugs] and I got pulled all over the place... because I was still so unsure about what I wanted and so unsure about myself...and I wanted to fit in.*
>
> *Diane: Mmmhmm.*
>
> *Sara: So if someone came and they seemed...nice and they said let's go, I would go.*

Diane: Yeah.

Sara: Because I wanted to be part of something, right?

Sara had told me that she used to be "really heavy into drugs." She had learned that to find a place to belong she had to adopt certain behaviours. Drug taking can be an affirmative action indicative of taking control of a situation. Youth may become part of a drug subculture as a response to being rejected by mainstream society. Unfortunately, in the subculture in which they feel acceptance, their acceptance is conditional on continued drug use. In our conversation, I saw Sara look to herself again and again for an explanation for why she became involved in drugs; she was so unsure of herself. 69

This practice, of viewing her experiences in a positive, uncritical light, continued when we discussed racism.

Diane: Somebody the other day [in a focus group discussion with other students] mentioned racism. Do you think that was a problem at your previous school?

Sara: Mmm, I didn't experience it so much. And people do say [name of school] is such an open school because there's these kinds of people and those kinds of people, but it's not really like that.

Diane: Mmmhmm.

Sara: It's like a mask. They show one thing but when you're on the inside of it it's not like that at all. And for me personally, I didn't experience any racism, but I know that there was you know, fights between this kind of group of people and another group from another school...but personally I didn't experience anything like that but I know that it happened. I heard lots of you know, mean things being said about people who had different sexual orientations and all that kind of stuff.

It was through this conversation that I discovered that Sara, like many students, considered racism to be overt, blatant acts that she herself didn't experience. But she also said that acceptance at the school was "like a mask." As well, her own experiences of rejection seem to support the idea that the school didn't meet her expectations. But what about the subtle racist leanings within the school, what about not seeing yourself in the images included in the school's TV program year-end show?

I think that Sara's attempts to survive in school and move out of the margins lead her to develop a survival method based on denial. As well, her powerlessness through "shyness" was affirmed because of the power relations between all members of the school. Understanding herself as "shy" was Sara's way of displacing, a way of surviving. Hers is a story of living in-between regimes of truth: her personal reality and the reality she hoped to achieve. The circumstances of her schooling thus took a large role in defining her "self" and how that "self" related to her larger community. How we view ourselves reflects the ways in which we view the world.

Sara's view of the world inside the school, as not really open and accepting, contributed to certain understandings about herself and the broader world around her. She reflected on her understandings of culture in her own life, saying:

> Sometimes you don't have like a...your culture is not that, mmm, important to your family, or something like that, so they don't teach you about those kind of things. Or like me, if you're mixed, then you just never learned anything about anything really, so it's kind of, and I kind of, I identify with what's there kind of thing. Because I am part Native so when I see Native dances or whatever I identify with that, and then other parts of me I don't really know anything about, right?

When she said this, telling me that her family didn't teach her much about "those kind of things," I wondered how prepared she was to resist the understandings of her culture provided by racist situations in her school. She was already experiencing difficulties at home and school, added to an absence of pride in cultural heritage. Feelings of low self-worth, complicated by economic and social disadvantage may have left her less resilient to racist comments she heard. Those who are more comfortable in schools and see their culture validated around them are clearly advantaged in building positive subjectivities. Race and class are built and build on each other in complex ways. Sara certainly didn't deny her mixed race, but she also said she didn't "know what my heritage really is." She knows one of her parents is Aboriginal and the other parent is black. She identified with what she was exposed to—Aboriginal elements of culture—but she had not yet explored her cultural heritage thoroughly, so she had not yet fully discovered the complex tensions between her "mixed-race" self and the more homogeneous power elite.

Speaking with Sara, and considering the complexities of poverty, race, and gender made me wonder how others may have felt in their public schools. All of the students at wrs found, like Sara, that schools aren't accepting places. Being defined by what you lack in relation to others heightens the desire to achieve precisely what is missing.

WHITE AND DISENFRANCHISED

MANY OF THE STUDENTS at wrs identify as white. I wondered how their "selfs" were formed in public high schools, what factors influenced them. I have read and engaged with literature on white privilege. I find much of it is relevant to me and my view of and position in the world, but I struggle to relate it to a population of disenfranchised urban youth. Some people have suggested to me that there is a difference between the Aboriginal and "mixed-race" youth and the white youth in my study of wrs. The white youth didn't experience racism along with the other forms of violence and neglect in their lives. While this is true, I have difficulty viewing a lack of racism as a "privilege." Clearly this "lack" should be a basic human right. So, I began to ask myself how the literature on white privilege could inform my analysis of white disenfranchised youth.

Most of the talk about white privilege assumes middle-class status as a starting point. The very notion of white privilege underscores a process many white people evolve through in the development of a white racial identity. Beverly Tatum, an African American psychologist who teaches about racism, outlines a process developed by Janet Helms, that she uses to help her understand the responses of white students in her classes.[2] The first stage is contact, best described as obliviousness. Being white is viewed as the "normal" state of being that is rarely reflected upon. The privileges associated with being white are therefore taken for granted. The state of obliviousness may, in the next stage, disintegrate, often because of increased interactions with people of colour. Greater awareness of "whiteness" is frequently accompanied by feelings of guilt, anger, and sadness that can be a catalyst for action (or denial). Finally, if the person chooses action, the stage of pseudoindependence follows, characterized by an intellectual understanding of the unfairness of racism as a system of advantage and a need to assume personal responsibility for dismantling that system.

This process sounds like one engaged in by people who have the knowledge and understanding to formulate these thoughts. It sounds academic. It sounds like the process I have gone through to become what Tatum calls a "white ally" or border person. Unfortunately, I have trouble locating disadvantaged urban youth in Tatum's process. They have continuous interactions with people of colour. Many of their friends are Aboriginal or "mixed race." But this didn't come about as the result of a change in lifestyle that led their paths to cross. They were always together, bound by the material conditions of their lives. One student, Ian, reflected on peer relations within WRS, saying, "The [public] school that I [attended] was very separated by all the races...[at] this school [WRS] everyone gets along because of their personalities."

They have always been friends, part of the same group. Still, it seemed to me that the white students would have had to be aware of their "whiteness." They knew they weren't victims of racial abuse in school, so they knew they were white. But what then is the cause of the abuse they did receive within their previous schools? How did their understandings of being ignored by teachers and socially isolated from peers affect how they constructed themselves? In reference to public-school teachers, one white youth, Carl, said they "might be a little bit more critical of things that happen and not understanding why you got into something [trouble] or whatever. That you're just a problem kid."

He knew himself as a "problem kid." Carl also displayed an understanding of the underlying causes of his behaviour when he indicated there was a *why* behind his behaviour. He was different from other youth who didn't cause "problems." When speaking with Carl, I was intrigued, and all kinds of questions popped into my mind: What else did he understand from his awareness that he was different from those who didn't cause problems? Did the youth who weren't "problem kids" share his socioeconomic background? Did they have difficulties at home? I asked him about racial problems in his former public school. He took a philosophical approach to answering the question, possibly in keeping with Tatum's first stage of identity development. He maybe didn't think the question applied to him directly, because he is a white person. He said, "There's a lot of prejudice in public schools, and I think it also comes because there's so many kids, you don't know each other as well, and with a separation like that it can actually, there can be a wall up between different groups and then each other, but they just know that they're different and there's a lot of prejudice that goes on just because of ignorance."

Carl noticed prejudice, but he attributed it to the size of the school he was at. Did he notice differences, like a hierarchy of group status in the school? Carl points to lack of understanding as a cause of "walls" being up between certain groups, but it's a *big* lack of understanding that does this. I wondered what all of this told him about himself and where he fitted in? Did he feel that he was at the top of the heap because he is white or at the bottom because he is poor? What happens to a white person's sense of self when he can see other white folks in positions of privilege while he isn't experiencing the same status? Even if he doesn't understand the academic concept of "white privilege," he can see it around him.

I wondered what stories Carl would tell to explain his lack of privilege to himself—what survival mechanism would he put into place to protect himself? Again, Carl pointed to school size: "With a lot of people there is like a lot of anonymity, you don't really feel like you really know anybody." Like Sara, Carl also adapted his behaviour to find a place of acceptance: "I kind of fell into the drug group, or whatever, and that kind of made it hard to go to school, and on top of that the lack of support from the teachers just made it almost impossible for me to learn anything at all. So I dropped out because I decided I just wanted to start working. I moved out of my mom's place."

In other words, Carl became a "druggie," which then informed his sense of self. Did it provide him with an explanation for his lack of privileged status? He said that it was the drugs that led him out of school. Lack of support from teachers was secondary to Carl. That is, he viewed his failure to complete school as being his own fault. At the same time, he showed me that he seemed to understand something about his social positioning based on family status when he said: "None of my family had even really finished high school. So I didn't really view university as any kind of a practical situation."

While he didn't talk at all about the fact that he is white, he did understand that he was poor. He didn't seem to understand that both of those factors combined to inform his sense of self in various ways. He knew what he wasn't. He clearly knew he was poor. What isn't apparent in his words is whether or not being white built his sense of self by increasing his status because he is not a person of colour *or* if it worked to point out his lack because he is not like the majority of white people. I think that likely some combination of both these ideas created tensions he had not yet resolved.

In recent years, critics and writers have begun looking at the combination of being white and being part of the working class and what that does to people in terms of self-building. Paul Willis's influential 1981 work, *Learning to Labor*, marks a beginning point for such investigations.[3] He paints an informative picture of white, working-class experience in an industrial city in the Midlands of Britain. As fine a sketch as Willis and other critics create of working-class whites, at WRS, a working-class identity is not relevant as the youth there are poor, many having shared experiences of abject poverty. However, Willis's work has enabled me to think about what class means at WRS and how it works. For example, the lads in Willis's work were often racist in their comments about other identifiable groups within the British working class. Willis points to three distinct groups—Caucasians, Asians, and West Indians—clearly visible in most school settings. The lads view group separation as rejection of others and, as noted, simply different colour can be enough to justify an attack or intimidation. Willis doesn't examine what this means for the lads, but clearly they see themselves in opposition to the racial others. They also believe that school staff supports them in their beliefs, whether or not they say so publicly. The truth of this statement matters little if the lads believe it to be true. It serves to validate their beliefs in the superiority of their own racial identities. The youth at WRS view separation between racial groups as largely negative as reflected in the comment above referring to a wall between groups. But similar to the lads, they, too, view themselves as in opposition to other groups—in their case based on economic advantage.

Other studies support the idea that social class is an important factor in a white racial identity. David Wellman, a professor at the University of California, Santa Cruz, discusses his experiences growing up in a black, working-class neighbourhood in Detroit and his coming to know himself as white when he entered a middle-class academic environment.[4] As a child of the only white family on the block, he knew he was white. His state of whiteness was never unknown to him, so he didn't go through Tatum's process in forming his white racial identity. In Wellman's neighbourhood, though, people didn't talk about his family's "whiteness" but instead talked about his parent's communist politics. This was a big deal in early 1950s in America. His family was known as the "Reds," the communists. Working class was normal, the unmarked category. As a child, Wellman knew he wasn't black, and, at the same time, as an adult, he knew was uncomfortable joining the white middle class. He points out that being defined negatively, as "not" someone else, does not convey the depth and complexity of experience or the richness and diversity of the self he has constructed.

Another author whose works I've visited is Lois Weis, who in her 2004 contribution to *Learning to Labor in New Times*, revisits the subjects of her earlier ethnographic investigation of white working-class female students and how identities are formed within complex relations inside schools.[5] While these female subjects currently hold full-time positions in the labour market, and most have realized their goals of not being wholly dependent on men, a significant proportion of them still experience abuse at the hands of men. Weis points out that these women have not been able to escape the violence associated with their working-class upbringing. She argues that it is conceivable that the physical cruelty of white working-class men becomes their last defensive resort in a world that has stripped them of alternative forms of power.

So, social class plays a significant role in the development of white youth. In a 2001 study of white girls from working-class and working-poor families, Lyn Mikel Brown found these girls were acutely aware of expectations that they should conform to idealized notions of white middle-class femininity, even as they lived within a different social class.[6] The contradictions between their lived experience and the expectations of middle-class teachers underscored their displacement in school and in white middle-class society. Against the idealized notions of femininity, the working-class girls' voices and behaviour didn't measure up. The behaviour that freed them from stereotypical gender conventions also labelled them as deviant.

When I began taking social class into account, I began to see a closer link between the disenfranchised white urban youth at WRS and those white working-class girls and boys who were part of the studies mentioned above. While there are still class differences between this group of youth and the working-class youth, some connections can be made. A look at individual lived realities sheds light on the depth and complexity of the experiences of disenfranchised urban youth at WRS. Is "social class" an unmarked category for WRS youth? As we have already seen, it appears that they *do* see social class and know that they are at the lower end of it. Yet, like Wellman, they are more comfortable being with others who share the material circumstances of their lives. How do they view the racial differences within their class at WRS and former public schools?

First, an Aboriginal perspective. One girl, Vicky, who had experienced a lot of racially-based "teasing" when she left her reserve school to attend school in a nearby city, said this to me about WRS:

Vicky: I came here and I like it.
Diane: And what do you like about it here?
Vicky: The students or the other people are easy to get along with and they accept you and all that.

Diane: Mmmhmm. So there isn't any problem here, I mean, here there's different people mixed together, too, right? There's some Aboriginal people, some white students—and that seems to work here?
Vicky: Mmmhmm. It works.
Diane: Everybody's accepting of each other.
Vicky: Yeah.
Diane: And do you have any thoughts on why that is, why it works well here, that mix of students?
Vicky: I don't even know.

While Vicky didn't indicate a deeper understanding of why the particular mix at WRS seemed to work well, she did reveal an understanding based on her earlier schooling experiences.

Vicky: On the reserves I never got teased. Only when I went to white schools, and that's when everyone started.
Diane: You say "teased," which isn't necessarily a negative word, but was it sort of joking teasing or kind of more nasty teasing?
Vicky: Yeah, more like mean, like trying to pull you down, and all that.

Vicky was definitely aware of racial differences and indicated that those racial differences were the cause of the abuse she'd received. Coming to WRS, she must still have seen those racial differences but she noticed that she was no longer a victim of abuse because of them. Racial differences do not appear as a negative to her in the context of WRS.

Students tend to get along at WRS regardless of skin colour. I firmly believe this is because they are bound together by poverty. Their similarities in social condition seem to isolate them from their differences. In this regard, Vicky revealed something else to me about her early schooling:

Vicky: I really liked the reserve school. It really made me feel comfortable, and all that. Because they were my people and they really made me feel at home, no one ever teased me or anything as I was growing up. My cousin was right in there, and I got close to everyone and that.

There's that word "comfortable" again. And her level of comfort didn't seem to be simply due to an absence of difficulties in school. She identified with "my people." She saw herself as like them. They were "family." The white schools made her feel uncomfortable, but then, so did some other aspects of her life.

> Vicky: My mom, she moved a lot, like they [parents] had problems and she always like took off, and I was just like stuck going with her and that.
> Diane: Mmmhmm. So how did you find schooling then when you were...
> Vicky: It was pretty difficult. It really like threw me off, like I could never stay in, like whenever I got stuck in one school and I was ready to go and all that and then she'd move back and I couldn't stay there any more.

Moving around was a problem for her like many of the youth at WRS I'd talked to. Family problems were something they had in common, as well.

> Vicky: I've always had like difficulties [in school] because I have problems at home and, like, I miss a lot of school because of that.
> Diane: Mmmhmm.
> Vicky: But...
> Diane: Is it better now that you're with your sister?
> Vicky: Mmm, yeah it's a little better. Yeah, because my mom, she used to just like drink and all that and it's not that good, but now I'm with my sister and it's alright now.

Although Vicky's perspective helped me to look at race- and home-related difficulties in public school, it was important for me to talk to white youth at WRS about the same matters. How do white youth view racial differences? What do the white youth say about the racial mix at WRS and why it seems to work? While not talking specifically to me about race, one white female student, Kelsey, and two white male students, Alex and Carl, said this about WRS.

Kelsey: If you're your own person they [other students] respect that.
Alex: Like the social structure is very strong. It's not, like [Kelsey] was
saying, two-faced...two-faced people. You're based on just who you are
and the way you act and respecting your own experience. And it's really
good that, you know, people appreciate everyone's space here and
everyone gets along.
Carl: [Teachers' names] they all come from fairly rough backgrounds.
So they really connect...the students and their problems...they treat you
like a person.

Kelsey, Alex, and Carl identified an atmosphere of respect that Vicky also talked about. They were talking to me about respecting others and "respecting your own experience," not just learning to like yourself in spite of all you have been through or done, but actually *respecting* your own lived reality. These students saw commonalities between *all* students in terms of coming from rough backgrounds. They identified with similarities and were not separated by differences. For these white youth, the racial differences of their public schooling experiences were now flattened out at WRS by socioeconomic similarities. Kelsey talked about how this process unfolded for her when she first arrived at WRS.

Kelsey: It was just before [name of former Aboriginal youth worker] left.
Diane: Was he helpful?
Kelsey: Yeah, he was great. He was joking around and stuff like that.
And he's the kind of a person that got me like actually liking the
environment and stuff like that. At first I was kind of worried because
I've had problems with Aboriginals in the past. Because I used to be
in [name of school with a high Aboriginal student population]. I was
like oh great, I'm going to get jumped...and everybody here was just
like, hey how's it going? And I was like, mmm, right, okay maybe I
shouldn't stereotype people anymore.

Kelsey went on to say that initially she "didn't want to talk to anybody" but "got more relaxed as time went on." In addition to a staff group that works to foster a sense of community, Kelsey talked about how, over time, students begin to look out for each other. They become protective of each other and their school, unlike what she experienced in public schools she had previously attended.

WHITE AND PRIVILEGED

I WONDERED HOW I fit into this school community. I have already talked about how being aware of my own white privilege has affected my work as a teacher and researcher. Beyond this, however, I must say that I have learned a great deal about myself from the youth I encountered while working at WRS. I have found that being conscious of my own experience as a white person has contributed much to how I understand the concept of "white privilege." I experience the world as a white person, and that world is built on the historical conditions of racism that situate white people in positions of privilege.

Personal experiences guide our actions as long as they are not contradicted by new and competing experiences. Knowing this has led me to consider what I once thought about my own racial identity. As a child and youth I viewed my whiteness as "normal" and only thought about it when I encountered people who weren't white in my predominantly white community. Other than the few Aboriginal families in town, the only other people who weren't white were children who had been adopted by white families. I think this scenario is an interesting one. Clearly the "normal" family unit in my experience was white—even for non-whites, since they were part of white families.

I recall when my older sister was in high school, her class had a student teacher who had earlier immigrated, with her family, from India. My sister and her friends were in awe of the beautiful young woman with the long black hair, who wore gorgeous, brightly coloured saris. She was definitely the exotic Other: a sight never before seen in our little town. What did she tell us about ourselves? I understood a universal concept of "whiteness" by learning a language for what wasn't viewed as normal. My understanding of North American "Indians" was now expanded to include "East" Indians. In relation to these Others, I was normal. White and middle class.

I didn't think about privilege as a child. I remember once complaining about the paleness of my skin when we were driving to the beach. My mother said, "When you are older you will appreciate it." Given that my mother was the one in my family who at least made an attempt to promote racial understanding, I understood her to mean that I would have an easier time in life being white than if I were not. So maybe I did think a little bit about privilege but only in the sense that privilege was normal. I certainly didn't think about structures in society that *allow* whites access to education, good jobs, and all the benefits those lead to. I didn't think about what it would be like to be the young Indian student teacher with all of us looking at her. I didn't have the language to formulate those concepts at the time.

For an experience to be valid and unquestioned, it must be constantly confirmed by other experiences. How did my field of vision become open to new experience? White as normal stopped being confirmed for me when I moved to Edmonton as a young adult, although even that process was slow. At first, I noticed people who weren't white, but they didn't directly affect my life so didn't challenge my assumptions in any significant way. But my image of normal was now imperfect. Things were not as I had previously thought. At this point, though, I still wasn't aware that whiteness might not be the norm. I only became conscious of other "normals" when I got to know a neighbour on a personal level. She was a woman who had come from India as a young child and grew up in northern Alberta before moving to Edmonton. Our children played together, and we spent a lot of time chatting as we kept a watchful eye on them. I began to understand that the *real* person I now knew was different from the assumptions I had previously held about Indian people. She was not what I had supposed her to be. Cultural practices, language, and race shape our interactions and experiences in the world, yet hopes, feelings, and desires remain remarkably alike. This experience was followed by many similar experiences that now confirmed a new *truth* about people who I had thought to be "different." This truth stood in opposition to absolute, repeatable knowledge and implied a process and openness to new experience.

After that, nothing returned to the way it was before. We are all experiencing our place in history unfolding. We are operating within a tradition, a language, that relates itself to us. The knowledge we acquire through the experience of language can be an understanding of another person. So what of the students at WRS? Authoritative teacher-pupil relationships rob students' claims on legitimacy, normalcy. I wondered, as a teacher, how I should ensure that I am not overlooking the youths' claims and allowing them to truly speak for themselves. As a white teacher and researcher, how should I become, and remain, open to the experiences of white youth and of non-white youth? The answer to this question, I think, lies somewhere and somehow in the readiness to experience. It is in the awareness that things are not naturally a certain way by virtue of having always been that way *for us*.

GENDER AND DISENFRANCHISED URBAN YOUTH

WE DO NEED TO REASSESS the implications of gender on disenfranchised urban youth. As is the case with the literature available on white privilege, books and studies done about gender often have middle-class subjects. To a certain extent, common experiences of homelessness, street involvement, violence, and abuse flatten out gender differences among youth. Similar to the ways in which racial differences are lessened by socioeconomic similarities, males and females are bound together in struggles to get by in harsh environments. In other respects, though, gender still makes a big difference in the lives of disenfranchised youth. The common experience of poverty sometimes has differing effects, depending on what your gender is.

The word "gender" is supposed to clarify our understanding of the social construct of sex. The practice of cheerleading in schools provides a perfect example of the construct of "feminine." Kelsey, both white and female, had some interesting thoughts about how gender is constructed.

The [cheer team] we had at [name of school], there was three white people on it. That's it...and the other girls didn't know what they were doing...they have their little head things or whatever, but that's like their religion...you're supposed to have your hair in ribbons...[they] couldn't wear the traditional [cheer team] uniforms.

For Kelsey, female gender was naturalized in the wearing of skimpy outfits and hair ribbons. She seemed to be saying that cheerleaders should dress and look a certain way. Those who are different, in this case Muslim, don't belong on cheer teams. And to fit this image it seems one has to be white, given her surprise at the relatively small number of white girls on the cheer squad. For the non-white girls on the cheer team, clearly culture and religion construct female gender in a different way. For them, cultural differences on a cheer team is a positive thing. Social class also informed Kelsey's thoughts and feelings about gender. For example, when she spoke to me about a different school she had attended, a school wherein many students were of a high economic status, she said that it, "has an awesome cheer team, everybody knows that." Commenting on the same school, though, she indicated a socioeconomic interpretation of those who were involved with cheerleading in the school when she said, "If you're not prep you're getting picked on."

Now it appears that those who form the cheer teams in schools are white, preppy, dressed in hair ribbons, and come from the middle class. Kelsey knew that even though she is white and female she did not belong in this group. "I left, and my friends slowly all left the school because it was changing."

When we talk about gender, we are referring to personality traits and behaviours, but we also increasingly invoke gender to differentiate social constructions that separate female bodies from male bodies. In this light, we don't see sex as separate from gender but controlled by it. Gender is the knowledge that establishes meanings for bodily differences.[7] Cross-cultural interpretations of gender cannot look to physical bodies for male–female distinctions. The human population differs in social expectations not only regarding how we think, feel, and act but also in the ways the body is viewed and the relationship between viewings and expectations. Culturally varied understandings of the human body do not remain constant over time. Linda Nicholson tells us the

tendency to think of sex identity as common cross-culturally is powerful and historically rooted in modern Western societies.[8] However, if we
can embrace difference, pointing out individual gender identities, we
can uncover the different "types" of gender that can allow women and
girls to better understand their social circumstances and, therefore,
their own bodies.

What seems to be important to understand about gender is the
complexity of the concept. The body is a historically specific variable
whose meaning and importance is recognized as potentially different in different historical contexts. We should develop the meaning
of "woman," for example, by looking at different meanings in different contexts. As well, we need to understand that how we choose to
represent a concept such as "woman" is emotionally charged and part
of a political struggle. For those who are disenfranchised, the idea that
"woman" is political raises questions regarding who has a voice in the
struggle. Who defines how the concepts of male and female are represented for those whose voices aren't heard? It seems that these young
men and women are defined by what they lack in terms of the middle-
class, mainstream ideals of gender.

In my work at WRS, I saw that there seemed to be differences
between Aboriginal, mixed race, and white youth in relation to gender.
I've already discussed the ongoing impact of colonialism and negative
images of Aboriginal people on Aboriginal youth, and of course racism
is a factor affecting the youth of colour at WRS. But Nicholson's interpretation of gender does not include those who are affected by poverty.
While conversations about understanding circumstances in social
terms do take place at WRS, disenfranchised youth have not had the
opportunity to develop such thoughts in their formal education, at that
privileged location of knowledge.

Leonard talked to me about a gender issue that grew out of personal
circumstances of violence and abuse, and this issue is a difficult one to
find in available writing on gender.

Leonard: I actually still see his [former student] sister when she...
Diane: She's on the streets...
Leonard: Yeah, she works on the streets. And it's a shame. It's a shame

because she was coming here for a little while, too, and she seemed
genuinely motivated to change that lifestyle. And then the same thing
happened. She disappeared and...
Diane: The obstacles are so great for them. You know, whereas working
the streets, there's money coming in, you're being taken care of...
Leonard: And they need the drugs, too, and, you know, to numb the
pain of the reality and, like my little sister's out there, you know. She's
working the streets out there. She has been for the past four years.

One of the girls Leonard was talking about is Aboriginal and the other is white. I wondered what their socially constructed interpretations of gender were. How did they see themselves as women? Did race come into the discussion? Certainly a conversation about race and intergenerational cycles of poverty and abuse would reveal some differences between how the two girls got to the streets of Edmonton, but does that really matter at this point? At a human level, they both suffer the effects of these intergenerational cycles. One also has to carry the additional burden of racism. Leonard offered this about the former student above and that student's sister: "Their foster parents were chronic alcoholics. They used to beat him and his sister all the time..."

So what now of gender? One of the students in question was male, the other female. In what ways did they experience this abuse differently? They seemed to follow the prescripts one finds in literature that highlights trends of boys being led into violent lifestyles selling drugs, and girls to work the streets as victims of violence. Being brought up in violent domestic environments affects males and females differently. Girls are much more likely to be arrested for running away from home, or for prostitution, than are boys. Girls are more likely to be sexually abused, and the abuse starts at an earlier age. The psychological stress girls feel resulting from these experiences tends to start at an early age and is often manifest in disruptive conduct in school. Running away from abusive environments and/or becoming involved in prostitution means facing judicial punishment from the authority personnel who were supposed to protect them from abuse, not contribute to it. Boys tend to engage more in violent behaviours resulting from environments that include parental conflict and parental aggressiveness.

The white male student Leonard talked about was a student in my class for a short time. Sam was a victim of parental aggressiveness and violence in the home. I worried about him, as did other staff members. Some mornings he was the only one in my class. We would just sit and talk, as he was obviously in pain. He would tell me he hadn't slept the night before because of the drunken party going on in his house. Sam would show me the "tattoos" he was carving into his arms with a pen. I listened, encouraged him to talk, and suggested we (teachers and youth workers) could help out with whatever he needed. Like his sister, he, too, disappeared, stopped coming to school. Last we heard he was selling drugs. So what of gender? How is "male" socially constructed in this context?

Much of the literature on gender not only assumes middle class but also assumes *female*. Males are supposed to be doing just fine, especially white males. But what if they aren't? As a male, Sam was supposed to be able to protect himself. He was supposed to have been able to protect his sister, as well. If he was unable to do so, the natural option would be to escape, physically by running away, and mentally by entering a world of drugs and alcohol. But how did he *feel* about himself as a result of all this? Certainly stress, antisocial behaviour, and depression correlate with stressors like physical or sexual abuse, having a parent with significant mental health or substance use disorder, and living in high-crime neighbourhoods. And a youth who carves his arms with a pen clearly doesn't feel very good about who he is as a person.

Then there was Sam's sister. I asked myself how does her story represent women, and how would she choose to represent herself? During adolescence, just as she was emerging as a person with her own thoughts, feelings, and desires, what did prostitution say to her about herself? In her 1989 book, *Runaway: Diary of a Street Kid*, Evelyn Lau reflects on her personal experiences as a prostitute.

> All my brain cells scream to ignore or deny what Roy is saying, but then it sinks in that he is right. The possibility has never struck me before; I'd always assumed that the men were the evil, disgusting creatures, that they were the ones hurting women, and especially prostitutes. But the

money I earned on the street wasn't for basic survival anymore, so who
was I to call myself pure?

In that one moment I realized that I was trash. I was a slut.[9]

While Lau reflects at length, in other parts of her diary, about the role
played by her emotionally abusive parents in leading her to run away,
she doesn't connect that understanding to this passage. She believes
she is trash because she is a prostitute. Her friend supports that
notion, as does the vast majority of the society in which she lives. What
started out as a way to survive, to take care of her self now tells her she
is "trash." Why is it that her position as a prostitute taking money that
helps her go beyond basic survival lead her to this conclusion? Why
can't she expect more for herself? Is it because she is trash that she
doesn't deserve the material comforts that others have?

Any conversation about prostitution leads to some interesting
thoughts about social expectations and the ways in which the prosti-
tuted body is viewed. Nicholson tells us that the term "gender" was
initially intended to supplement the term sex. If the physiological self
was the "location for establishing where specific social influences are
to go" then the "relationship between biology and socialization makes
possible what can be described as a 'coat-rack' view of self-identity."[10]
The body can be viewed as a type of rack upon which "differing cultural
artifacts, especially those of personality and behaviour, are thrown."[11]
This concept of "throwing" behaviour and personality onto a body is
interesting in relation to prostitution. A coat rack is a stand fitted with
hooks, which we use for hanging clothes. It is something to be used,
similar to a prostitute's body. Cultural artifacts of street life, such as
drugs, violence, and disease, can be thrown onto the rack. I feel that we
need to rethink the meaning we give to the female body in this context;
and to do this we need to try to grasp complex historical and contemporary societal conditions.

Nicholson does clarify the understanding of gender as a coat rack
with behaviours thrown on, as one that is rooted in a worldview common
to the early modern period in Western Europe and North America,

where biology was seen as the basis of social distinctions. Now, we need to consider a diverse set of meanings in order to see the complexity of gender. We need to consider historical conditions related to social class and race relations in Canada. We need to see gender differences as affecting the criteria of what it means to be a man or a woman in diverse societies. What does it mean to be a woman on the streets of inner-city Edmonton? When you "sell" your body for sex in order to survive, how do you view your body? How do we give meaning to the female body in this time and place? It seems to me that the disenfranchised body is the site of a struggle to maintain dignity, to find ways to protect against physical harm, and for a self-identity that doesn't require drug-induced escapism. Gendered students within disadvantaged groups go against a norm that says the behaviour of prostitution is morally repugnant and those who engage in this behaviour (disenfranchised female victims of abuse) are trash.

I have chosen to present a particular profile of gender here. While the prostitute gender is certainly not an uncommon profile of the disenfranchised urban youth that come and go from WRS, there are many other "gendered" students within the school. For example, Sara, a young mixed-race woman, talked with me about her need for acceptance and how she let her boyfriend dictate her behaviour: "I let those people [boyfriends] kind of direct my [life] and I should have been directing my own. And for awhile I did really good, because you know those people weren't around, maybe they went to jail or whatever."

Sara's desire to be accepted by her boyfriend, who is also the father of her child, created a dependency that influenced her choices. She talked about how he didn't want her to go to school and about her spiral into drug dependency when she was with him. Engaging in drug use and related behaviours made her feel that she was a "really bad druggie." Knowing that her boyfriend was the only person she had to depend on may have been what made her think that: "I just find it hard to communicate with other people." As a woman, she learned that she needed to depend on a man and that she was bound by the restrictions he placed on her behaviour if she wanted to remain with him.

The thoughts and feelings reflected in the words of these students reveal a greater complexity of the concept of gender when applied to disenfranchised urban youth. As they come to know themselves as gendered subjects they struggle with conflicting images of who they are and who they desire to be. An understanding of how social location affects subjectivity is important for both youth and those who strive to help them move forward in their lives.

FEMALE AND MIDDLE CLASS

I CAN ALSO USE THE "coat rack" analogy to talk about my own gender 89 as a middle-class woman. In order to understand your students, you must try to understand yourself.

I tried to disguise my female body as a male throughout most of my childhood. I wore my hair short and dressed in boys' clothes. I was a tomboy. I wanted to be like my older brother. I knew he was my father's favourite. It was better to be a boy. Everyone knew that. You could pee in the bushes when you were out playing. While clearly my father contributed to my desire to be a boy, he wasn't the only social influence in my life. In small-town Manitoba in the 1960s and 1970s, women were homemakers and men worked outside of the home. If you happened to be educated like the one female physician in town, you could get away with working part-time, but, otherwise, women who worked were "working class." There were whisperings that these women *had* to work outside the home. Even the idea of "outside the home" is a more recent understanding. It was more common for us as kids to say, "My mother doesn't work," or "My mother stays home." What did she do? Did she sleep all day? No one knew. We weren't at home to notice.

This norm has to be understood within the context of time and place. The idea of middle-class, urban, white women staying home to tend to children and the house was promoted as an ideal following the Second World War in Canada. It quickly became a status symbol. It was a sign that a man could look after his family if his wife "stayed at home." My mother had a university degree in interior design, but she aspired to be a good housewife. When my parents both passed away, my sister and I sorted through their "stuff" in an attempt to empty the family home and sell it. We found stacks of *Good Housekeeping* magazines, recipes, menus, and journals outlining plans to make house and home a shin-ing example of domestic bliss. Clearly at one point in time my mother had hoped for a career, but something changed, resulting from societal messages she received. And children can read certain messages from their parents' actions about whether or not a woman can or should have a career. They also receive messages about whether or not a woman is capable of looking after herself.

Being male was normal at that time, something to aspire to. It was in my tomboy behaviour, and, it also manifested in the behaviours of women as they began to leave the home and enter the public realm of work. These working women seemed to be saying, "We can be just like men (in spite of our weaker female bodies)." This period of denial was followed by two decades of feminist political activism and scholarship in a variety of sociopolitical and geographical locations. We are now in a new period of *feminization* characterized by the rise of women's eco-nomic power and self-invention by women in the new labour market.[12] While the opening up of jobs to women offers exciting possibilities for women it also brings the double burden of work and family.

LEARNING FROM LISTENING

I DON'T REALLY THINK of family as a burden. While recognizing that I have taken on a disproportionate share of childcare, as well as a career, I also am blessed with three wonderful children who provide me with an opportunity to reflect on what children should be. That is, well taken care of, loved, loving, happy, caring, and giving. I want all of these things for the youth at WRS.

I learn from my children, and I also learn from the WRS youth. I have learned that young girls who work the streets and young boys who sell drugs and live violent lives are people. They are individuals with their own claims to legitimacy. I once viewed street life through a middle-class lens, seeing "prostitutes" and "drug dealers." In so doing, I robbed them of their voices, judged them, and failed to understand them. A turning point in the way I viewed and understood "prostitutes" and "drug dealers" came during the time I spent talking with Sam in the quiet, empty classroom. Things I had read and thought I under-stood now came alive as I got to know this youth on a personal level. Talking to Sam helped me to understand other youth, as well, to *really* listen to what they had to say, without judging them. The next step for me was to *value* what they had to say, to incorporate their lived experi-ences into the classroom.

The places where poverty, race, and gender meet inform the ways in which "selfs" are formed in schools. How disenfranchised urban students are made to feel about themselves are central to their inclina-tion to leave public-school environments. While disadvantaged youth tend to take personal responsibility for their lack of academic and social success in schools, my analysis of conversations with them reveals to me the understandings they have about how poorly they are treated in schools.

In addition, I have learned through conversation that the idea of "white privilege" is not really relevant when applied to disenfranchised urban youth. These youth comprehend whiteness differently; they view it through a lens of material and social disadvantage. At the same time, although there are differences between the ways in which males and females experience difficult social circumstances, they also share disenfranchisement. They are all touched by violence, hunger, home-lessness, and prejudice.

UNDERSTANDING THE REAL person behind the labels of prostitute, drug dealer, disenfranchised urban youth, or problem kid are crucial to giv-ing young people a voice. I believe it is essential for teachers to create conditions for dialogue that encourage students to be conscious of the social and societal conditions of their lives. Such conversations may lead to them feeling a degree of comfort they did not experience in public schools.

OTHER TENSIONS:
SCHOOLS, TEACHERS, AND STUDENTS

Educators have developed categories and modes of perception which reify or thingify individuals so that they (the educators) can confront students as institutional abstractions rather than as concrete persons with whom they have real ties in the process of cultural and economic reproduction.[1]

THE WAYS IN WHICH we treat and view students as "objects" in schools prevent us teachers from successfully intervening in our students' academic lives. When we begin to talk about the tensions within teachers in schools, however, a many-headed beast rears up, each head representing an opposing force that is rife in schools. Instead of being immobilized by the spectre of this beast, I think we can try to understand the stresses between school systems, teachers, and students by being aware of historical and current theoretical and pedagogical struggles in schools. This study of WRS, an example of this struggle in a contemporary context, will add to literature already out there about different schools and challenges that teachers face. The particular tension felt by teachers and students alike when students are viewed as objects and not people is the one I hoped to delve into when beginning my study of the school.

THE DANGERS OF LABELLING

WHILE MANY TEACHERS and youth workers at WRS have keen insight into the realities of street life and the needs of the youth who come to their school, meeting these needs is not a straightforward process. These youth have been through many years of school, social, and justice systems that have labelled them in various ways. And, as James said, "When someone's been told for so long that they're not smart and that they can't do it, they begin to believe that themselves."

We *know* labels are dangerous. We've known this for years. That's why we stopped "streaming" students into separate schools and programs. Yet labels are still around, and, to be honest, so is streaming. We now call streaming "choice," and new labels, such as "academic" and "non-academic," are designed to "help." These labels, supposedly designed to assist teachers to meet students' learning needs, hide the unique circumstances and processes between people through the use of a neutral language that disguises the social and economic conditions of those so labelled. By continuing to favour conditions within which young people become abstractions, we as teachers cease to see students as persons. And in the end, we fail to understand the impact of the ways in which we construct youth, and of how youth understand themselves outside of the labels.

First and foremost, I think teachers need to recognize that the categories we file youth into are themselves social constructs. That is, we are creating categories that grow out of middle-class-value-laden judgments about what youth *should* be, and then we use those very labels as a way of denying and devaluing the people they really are. Meg, an early service teacher at WRS, pointed out to me, "I've never worked with this population of people ever and like coming from where I've come from is very different...I have come from a very comfortable lifestyle."

Meg recognized social class differences between herself and the disenfranchised urban youth she was teaching, but she failed to comprehend how these differences affected the ways in which she interpreted the youth in her classes. She went on to say, "I think [name of student] is lucky 'cause she has some of that classiness, there's [something in her] that she's actually a positive kid and wants to do something [be a positive influence on her siblings]. But the other stuff gets in the way... she doesn't want to go back to jail." So in order to have "classiness" (definitely a middle-class label) you have to be "positive." A "positive kid" is one who wants to help her siblings, stay out of jail, and do something with her life. For this teacher, this is what a youth should be like. At the same time, Meg seems to be saying that "this population of people" by their very nature could not possibly hold such middle-class values.

Her words spoke to me as a teacher. I was already familiar with what she was saying about disenfranchised youth as I, too, entered this school environment with middle-class values firmly entrenched. I, too, come from a comfortable lifestyle. I was implicated by her words, as I had once had the same biases. I *was* that teacher and was complicit in imposing similar social constructions on students. Thinking about what she said to me that day made me realize how language serves to rout us out, to expose our true beliefs and understandings. We can quite easily learn to talk the talk, perhaps saying that we don't "label" youth, but walking it means we have to make deep, fundamental changes to the way we think about the world.

Teachers have the power to label students and insert them into specific social roles. Some students are "academically advanced" while others are "at-risk" of "early school leaving." I have chosen to use the term "disenfranchised" when I talk about the students who attend WRS, which is also not a neutral term. Of course, it is difficult to talk about *groups* of students without using some sort of label. When I spoke to James about the double-edged sword of labelling, he said, "I think there's room at the university for a minor in—I know that there's a lot of controversy, that they're youth at risk, but call them whatever you want—high-need youth or youth who have had difficulty in the traditional system, but it's a problem and I personally believe there should be a minor...but at the very least there should be a couple courses that student teachers are required to take...there should be some understanding." James understood there are problems with labels, but what *do* you call this group of youth?

I think the biggest problem rests in the use of the labels. In this context, the greatest danger to students happens when teachers apply classifications to students regardless, uncritically, without an awareness of the assumptions behind the labels and the ways in which they construct (and often hurt) youth. When teachers do this, they are treating the labels they apply as commonsense tools rather than as historically constructed products of institutions and social conditions.

If we can gain insight from being critical about the labels we use in schools, it is at least a first step away from the damaging effects of enforced middle-class values. The term "at risk," for example, has been used uncritically for a number of years and continues to be used in the absence of another more definitive term, hence my use of the term "disenfranchised." As I have built this story of WRS, the concept of "at risk" has become significantly striking to me; the term has become a microcosm of all dangerous labels that has urged me to further understand labelling in a more general sense, as well as its consequences.

ORIGINS OF THE TERM "AT RISK"

COMING TO APPRECIATE the lives and circumstances of those *most* "at risk" made me question the many ways in which this term has been used. At my daughter's middle-class elementary school an "at-risk" discourse was adopted in response to government funding cutbacks to schools, to point to the needs of those students who weren't reading at grade level in early primary grades. No other risk factors were seemingly apparent, and it is questionable whether not reading at grade level in these first few years of school is a risk factor at all for these children. So the school was using an available and accepted discourse to further its aims for additional funding in a school that was already at the top of the testing hierarchy. This experience led me to question commonsense notions I had held and the ways in which teachers in middle-class schools usurp words that were initially used in the system to address the needs of those living in impoverished communities. Having class advantage enabled my daughter's school to further the class advantage, at the expense of those who were disadvantaged. This school had the ability to secure additional funding, dollars that should have gone to a needier school with an actual "at-risk" student population. While I previously saw the advantages my own children had, I came to understand some of the structures in place that further enhance those advantages.

In 2001, Alberta Learning used the term "at risk of leaving school early" to describe students who were disenfranchised and coping with complex problems in their lives.[2] As recently as 2006 this same government department was still referring to "students at risk of leaving school."[3] According to Terry Wotherspoon and Bernard Schissel in their article, "The Business of Placing Canadian Children and Youth 'At-Risk,'" educators have only relatively recently been labelling learners as "at risk," "disadvantaged," or "marginalized," but identifying students as having "disabilities" or "special needs" has been going since the early part of the twentieth century.[4] The authors link the use of these terms in schools with changing visions of what is "normal" since the 1870s. They suggest that such labels arose out of educators' desires to provide opportunities for educationally disadvantaged youth, as well as minimize the problems these learners pose for the other students in the classroom who are not seen to be "at risk."

Wotherspoon and Schissel, in a review of literature, identified 450 symptoms experienced by school-aged children deemed to be "at risk."[5] No wonder we have trouble valuing these children as people. In 1995, the Organisation for Economic Co-operation and Development (OECD) identified children and youth "at risk" as those who come from disadvantaged backgrounds where poverty is a frequent common factor. While teachers know that "at risk" is a multi-dimensional concept, we also are aware of poverty as a common underlying cause. When we talk about "at-risk" students, we're not talking about the middle class, the class to which most educators claim membership. What ends up happening with labels that are applied by one class onto another, is that the labels only serve to strengthen the class that does the labelling, rather than reduce the "risk" of those so labelled. We can see that children and youth living in poverty are often lumped together under the label "at risk," but this label includes others who have been marginalized and denied access to educational opportunities. Who else are we teachers working to "save" in ways that allow us to feel good about our own privileged positions in the mainstream of education?

At WRS Aboriginal youth are also considered "at risk." In fact, throughout Alberta, if a student has been labelled "at risk" he or she is probably also Aboriginal. Many of the youth at WRS are deemed to be *doubly* "at risk"—both poor and Aboriginal. Recently, in conversation with an Aboriginal graduate student in my department at the University of Alberta she pointed out that as a general rule every child in the detention room in her son's school is Native. I believe that this language of "risk" can serve in schools as a crutch for racism, sexism, and other biases. Labelling Aboriginal students "at risk" makes it okay to send them to the detention room. In a recent study by Diane Conrad, a drama educator at the University of Alberta, youth, many of whom were Aboriginal, found the label "at risk" to be offensive.[6] No doubt, if the term means Aboriginal, and Aboriginal means detention.

The term "at risk" came into widespread use in the public school system relatively recently and was meant to point to the failures and limitations of public education. The label has since come to represent either failures of public education to contribute to the economic advancement of society as a whole or commitment to policies that facilitate the aims of inclusive schooling. There is a tension here between meeting societal needs and meeting the needs of the individual student. We have difficulty meeting the needs of students who are "at risk" in schools because their very presence disrupts goals of economic advancement. The issue has become this: How do educators best meet the needs of those who are educationally disadvantaged while simultaneously viewing these same students as disruptions in the classroom? Who is at risk? The school or the child?

Labelling students who disrupt the status quo in schools is a way of helping us avoid those who are disadvantaged and focus instead on the broader goals of public schooling. If we teachers are supposed to be connecting with our students' lives, how can it be that acceptable outcomes in schools, as measured by the instruments of coding, highlight *avoidance* of behavioural problems? And how do we avoid "behaviour problems" *without* connecting with the lives of learners? These questions beg teachers to come to a new understanding of labelling and its consequences.

THE INSTITUTION AND THE ECONOMY
How and Why Alberta Produces and Supports Labelling and "Treatment"

MICHAEL APPLE OUTLINES the ways in which the abstract labels that grow out of institutional life become quite serious.[7] If a teacher can identify a student as having "special needs" or *being* "special needs," she can then prescribe general treatments that are assumed to be neutral and helpful. Since categories like "special needs" are defined by institutional abstractions, the teacher doesn't have to examine the *context* that defined the label in the first place. Most of the time, teachers assume that the label is neutral and that the child belongs in it. The "treatments," in turn, protect both the existing institution and the teacher from questioning both the label and the reality of the "special" child. For example, when recording anecdotal information for those who have been coded (42) at WRS, the form I used in my class allowed for documenting of particular behaviours that were inappropriate and the specific adult response that was designed to help the student develop more socially appropriate behaviours. Results were measured by the student's compliance to requests by staff. The reasons behind the behaviour are not explored in relation to this treatment.

Since 1990, the label-treatment process has evolved in Alberta.[8] At that time the provincial government reviewed the inclusion of students with "special needs." In 1991, the Minister of Education announced that schools would be focusing on integrating students with "special needs" into the "regular" classroom. In 1994, general reductions in spending for public education adversely affected these attempts at integration. As a result of changes in school funding, schools wishing to access funds for "special needs" students now had to go through a rigorous application process. For example, a grant was made available for severe disabilities funding. Students with severe emotional/behavioural disabilities are funded based on chronic or extreme behaviours requiring constant adult supervision and intensive support services in order to function in an educational setting.

Many students at WRS have an emotional/behaviour coding of (42), which means:

A clinical diagnosis within the last 2 years of a severe emotional/behavioural disorder by a psychiatrist, chartered psychologist or a developmental pediatrician is required, in addition to extensive documentation of the nature, frequency and severity of the disorder by school authorities.[9]

At WRS, youth who are coded (42) are also diagnosed with Oppositional Defiant Disorder or Antisocial Personality Disorder, and it must be proven that this disorder causes severe detriment to their learning environment for funding to be accessed. The school must not only demonstrate that there is a current detriment to the classroom, but it must also present a documented history of detriment. The behaviours that serve to interfere with the learning environment include: hostility and disobedience toward authority, acts or threats of violence, destroying others' property, lying to and manipulating others, and violating rules. Funding for this code is dependent upon the documented range, frequency, and impact of these negative behaviours on the school.

The labels that define WRS youth, as having special needs understood as severe emotional/behavioural disabilities, arise out of an institutional context that views middle class as the norm. Behaviours that are *different* are labelled *disabilities*. As James told me, "The problem is that the skills that they've learned to survive in their environment are actually a trap that keeps them in their environment, and they're [these skills] not conducive to academic success at all."

Clearly we have failed to recognize potential for academic development, and we've also failed to understand the environmental context of the lives of these youth. Again, I, too, had accepted the assumptions regarding *inability* to perform well in a formal classroom context as an early service teacher at WRS. Teaching *these* youth in *this* context revealed something new, however. The environment outside of school is important to both teaching and students' academic success. Reflecting on teaching practice with these students makes it possible for teachers to shed their biases and adopt a new understanding of disenfranchised youth, one that is important in keeping a conversation going between the teachers and the youth. This conversation is necessary to help us teachers better understand a segment of a population that is currently underserved by schools.

My work at WRS made me wonder what brought us to this current understanding of special needs categories in schools. Educational researchers may be lending the abstract prestige of science to what may be questionable educational practices related to special needs funding.[10] The problem rests here. Clinical language, such as "severe emotional and behavioral disability," is really none other than another label, albeit one that confers scientific status to "helping" the disenfranchised. We have created a process in which youths' behaviours are deconstructed, rules for interpreting these behaviours are developed, and solutions are constructed based on the rules. In our attempts to control and predict, we objectify youth and separate them from their environment, an environment that gives meaning to who they are. While we may think that this process helps us to "know" our students better, it only protects us from being exposed to something new in the world. It also protects us from understanding real people in real contexts.

Now who is "at risk"? It is *us*, teachers and other educators, who are at risk of *understanding*—at risk of knowing what our actions are doing to the youth who need us most. But not following the rules might disrupt the status quo, which we teachers benefit from. But perhaps there is yet another entity that is also "at risk."

You have to appreciate the larger economic context in Alberta in order to fully understand "at-risk" labelling and its consequences. The basis for "at-risk" language and policies arise out of an *economy* that is "at risk" of not being well-prepared to compete globally. The Alberta Government Annual Report reminds us that an excellent education system is an excellent investment in the future.[11] This statement reflects the province's attempt to raise high-school completion rates as a necessary goal in the face of global competition. To this end, Alberta Learning's "Removing Barriers to High School Completion" report notes their business plan has set a target for improving high-school completion in order to create conditions for investing in Alberta.[12]

Students who fail to complete high school also fail to contribute to the economy and, ultimately, to maintain an Alberta that is attractive to international investment. This is how students become an abstraction, a missing piece in the province's desire to compete on the global stage. At the same time, Albertans' global competitiveness is not the focus in relation to *students* who fail to complete. Instead, educators pay attention to "at-risk" students' specific behavioural, emotional, or educational "problems," thus diverting attention from the inadequacies of the educational institution itself and the conditions that caused the necessity of applying these constructs in the first place. In most Alberta schools, the need to compete globally is uncritically adopted as necessary, as is the place of disenfranchised youth within it. The educational institution itself has become a cog in the wheel. While we teachers often witness tensions between social justice and social control in schools, we also see the ways in which labelling *produces* youth "at risk" by constructing them as problems.

WRS AS AN ALBERTA INSTITUTION

WRS SENIOR TEACHERS SEE how teacher education programs do their part to train teachers who will be ready to impart the competitive global spirit into their students. James told me:

> [New] teachers don't know how to respond to the students [at WRS] and they respond in ways often that are not helpful...teachers are trained to be in charge and to be bosses. Unfortunately most of these students that we have had too much of that...it drives them out the door. And other times teachers will want to get into well, "You didn't complete the assignment, I'm sorry, you fail." That's standard practice because how can you do otherwise when you have a class of thirty or thirty-five students? You're moving through the curriculum and you have to meet the demands of all those parents and the administration, and you have to get through the course. That's the training that they bring with them here, and responding in a different way seems less than professional to them.

New teachers coming out of teacher education programs view a particular approach to teaching as necessary. Being in charge, a banking style of teaching, allows for students to move rapidly through the curriculum. When classroom activity does not unfold as they believe it should, these teachers express frustration. As Meg said to me, "I'm still struggling with this, like Science 10 where they come and they come back and they go and they come back, and I get pissed off because we don't have any of their stuff and they expect you to drop what [you] are doing and go, like [student's name]; it's driving me wild right now. So that's a transition, 'cause usually in all the schools I've been at, even through teaching, [the process is] there's the papers, find it, get somebody to help you."

Meg, new to WRS, was referring to the inconsistent attendance patterns that are common to the school and the ways in which most schools foster independence in students.

As a teacher new to WRS, I, too, was often frustrated when students reappeared without the course materials I had already provided. I recall one student in particular who regularly told me he had spilled coffee on his papers and wanted me to make new copies for him. I wondered why he didn't quit drinking coffee if it was causing such a problem. But the problem is not that. The problem is if you have no regular home or someone regularly expressing an interest in your schooling, keeping track of your *school things* is not a big priority. By speaking with teachers new to WRS, I found out that on some level new teachers understand this. Annie, for example, told me, "If you had a kid who from kindergarten to grade nine has had nobody say to them, 'You know, you are smart, you can do this, keep trying, you will get it.' They're not getting it from home; they're not hearing that from their mom and dad. They need some sort of reward system."

The new teacher's belief, however, is that these students are lacking the "skills" needed to function in an academic setting. By implementing a reward system, we as teachers can help them overcome this lack. We can bring them up to the *appropriate* standards expected in a school. Like learning to take responsibility for your things. It is interesting to note that "things" (material), and looking after them, are important in schools and that we have come to view "special needs" students as "things" (objects), also needing to be managed. Students, like pencils, papers, and assignments, come to be seen as another set of cogs in our materially based, at-risk economy.

At first, teachers new to WRS demonstrate little awareness of the assumptions being made about values, such as looking after one's things, or about *these* students and the skills they lack. We know that these youth do not fit the profile of what is *normal* in schools. That is why they are coded as (42), complete with severe emotional and behavioural disabilities. But "coding" is a problem. As I mention above, the institution of schooling labels these students as such, primarily because of the assumptions of normalcy held by school personnel.

Following a conference presentation on the difficulties the process of coding poses for schools like WRS, a woman who had been in the audience approached me to discuss her concerns with the information being collected in the interests of diagnosing "special needs" students. She identified herself as a lawyer who had done some work with the Alberta Government *Freedom of Information and Protection of Privacy Act* (FOIP). She asserted a concern that the government was asking for too much information, more than they need, which is in violation of the spirit of the act. Documenting "numbers" of observed behaviours tells us little about the reasons behind the behaviours. Coming away from my conversation with her, I had to ask myself: Why *does* the government need to know how many times the students in my class swear in an hour? I also wondered why these actions are considered emotional and behavioural *disabilities*, rather than *learned* behaviours.

I think that the "neutral" language of coding, disabilities, and special needs relies upon tentative and incomplete data, and teachers may apply the language to students inappropriately. Is it appropriate to count swear words (and other behaviours) and use this information uncritically to assess a person's mental wellbeing without understanding environmental circumstances? And then use this assessment to control behaviour? My chance conversation with the lawyer at that conference opened me up to looking at coding in a different way than I had previously. An assumption was broken open. Just because the government asks for and collects information doesn't mean it is *necessary* information or even that it is being used. My experience challenged my beliefs and pointed to my complicity in a system of "experts" who have the *right* answers. What are the right answers and what are the right questions? How did the questions come to be about behaviours? My chance conversation has led me to think that what has been said about "special needs" in the past needs to be rethought by teachers by exposing them to thought-provoking pedagogical situations, like the one at WRS.

By focusing simply on *behaviours*, educators can conveniently label students in ways that are acceptable within the institution of schooling and in the wider community. While government authorities may not be using all the data collected in the interests of coding students, the very act of teachers collecting the information affects both teachers and students: teachers in their understanding of their students and the way they teach them; and youth in the way they view themselves. We as teachers have come to accept the *expert* opinion uncritically with little understanding of underlying political aims or ethical consequences. We believe we are helping or, at least, that those "special needs" students are being helped. Coding has allowed us to feel good about ourselves and our teaching. We feel that something is being done for and about those poor unfortunate souls. But in the process students are being stereotyped in ways that allow us to deal with the stereotype instead of the individual.

In the end, by accepting coding practices as they stand at face value, teachers are refusing to challenge the dominant values of society, the status quo. What coding tells us is congruent with what we already understand. We start to believe that the behaviours of disenfranchised urban youth must be pathological because they are inconsistent with the behaviours of the youth we know, youth from the dominant classes. As I result, I think that we need to challenge the statistics that are based on these official labels and categories, using new knowledge: that ideological assumptions underpin the constructs within which the data was generated. In the end, we need to rethink the assumptions that define emotional and behavioural disabilities in schools.

STRUGGLES TO DE-CODE

STUDENTS AT WRS HAVE endured many years of teachers who have labelled them in various ways. These youth know the ways in which teachers and peers understand them. The labels shape students' understandings of themselves, whether or not the labels are formally applied.

As was earlier noted, the process of coding is a process of objectifying youth. Given that new teachers to WRS are playing an active role in coding behaviours as pathological, I have wondered in what ways WRS practices attempt to reshape these teachers' understandings of disenfranchised youth as active subjects. I went to the teachers to find out.

Senior staff members at WRS tend to fault teacher education programs as not adequately preparing teachers for a context that necessitates meeting the needs of disenfranchised urban youth. The reality, however, is that WRS's students have specialized needs that require teachers to give up their assumptions. Reflecting on this, James said, "It's good for us because we get young teachers, first year or so, because they're not totally set in their ways, somewhat malleable, and we can work with them easier."

But working with new teachers to reshape impressions and judgments is a long process, and often the new teachers aren't committed enough to see the process through. While many of the staff team comprehend the difficulties inherent in the lives of WRS students and are keen to contribute to their education, some teachers are there simply because they can't get *better* jobs in the public system. As James said, "I think a lot of the times it's people looking for a job because they have to pay the rent or pay the mortgage, and that's usually when it's difficult for us. I think what we should be doing is paying people above grid, and we should have teachers who are here because they're interested in the kind of challenges that are here."

Teachers whose minds aren't open to new ways of looking at disenfranchised youth are certainly going to be more influenced by the messages of the coding process than the counter-messages being presented in staff meetings and via general school philosophies. In this way, at WRS, the coding practice and the values of the school clash constantly.

All staff members are actively involved in discussing common problems and fostering solutions at weekly staff meetings. One frequent problem that new teachers relate are the "stories" many youth present that are a reflection of the manipulation tools, such as getting away with things and being tough, that they have learned in order to survive on the streets. James said, "We have weekly staff meetings where we discuss each student in the school. And then each staff member has input into that discussion. The threads of manipulation are exposed in that process."

The staff meeting serves other purposes, as well. It provides a forum to reflect on teaching practice and solicit input on solving problems in the classroom, a platform for working toward collective responses to school-wide concerns, and a supportive environment to share the burdens of listening to and dealing with students' painful experiences on an ongoing basis.

By talking to new teachers at WRS, however, I found out that their impressions of the staff meetings weren't always positive. Meg said, "I tune out sometimes. I do get frustrated 'cause I wanna get done and I tend to be that way in general...I find myself organized, but I'm also quite social so it doesn't bother me. At the start of the year it bothered me when we were here until five o'clock."

Meg sees the meetings as disorganized and dragging on far too long. As a teacher, I sat through many of these meetings, and they can certainly appear to be simply rambling conversation. But, how can a meeting that hopes to provide such a forum for teachers adhere to a tightly timed agenda? While new teachers slowly come to understand the student population through this process, they do not always understand the importance of the process itself.

Talking to Meg made me reflect on how I came to understand the relevance of the process at WRS and how much my formal education may have contributed to my understandings.

When new teachers don't grasp or embrace the value of staff meetings, is it because the potential benefits haven't been adequately impressed upon them, or is it that they reject these benefits? As James said, "It's difficult working with new teachers because they know their job or they wouldn't have their degree." James sensed resistance. He went on to tell me that if new teachers had been exposed to the possibility of WRS students within their university program they would not be so resistant to new processes and ways of educating when they encountered an unfamiliar teaching environment.

Richard, a youth worker, agreed with James's impression of new teachers: "The problems with the teachers, if the staff is working as a team and we're all sort of on the same level and we're used to doing the same things, when somebody new comes in there's sort of adjustments and misunderstandings, and I find it complicates it, makes it hard for the whole team that's operating."

At WRS teachers are expected to be part of a team that includes youth workers. Everyone works toward a common goal. The teacher's thoughts and beliefs now need to be shaped by more than just their solitary status inside the classroom. It seemed to me that early service teachers were not developing an appreciation of the structural differences of school operations or their changed role within these structures. I, too, needed to have someone explain school operations to me. But, what is different about this school for *the teachers?* My conversations with early service teachers made me think that they didn't necessarily find value in school practices. Rather, they believed the school and its inhabitants needed to be fixed.

TAKING A CLOSE LOOK at schools like WRS can give us a glimpse of what schooling for disenfranchised youth might look like if it were informed by an understanding of environmental circumstances rather than a scientific discourse. What follows is an example of school practice that challenges the status quo by questioning the categories students have been placed in and bringing their lives outside of school into the classroom.

UNDERSTANDING SCHOOL PRACTICES AND CRITICAL LITERACY

Educators need to know what happens in the world of the children with whom they work. They need to know the universe of their dreams, the language with which they skillfully defend themselves from the aggressiveness of their world, what they know independently of the school, and how they know it.[1]

HOW DOES A SCHOOL that is challenging how disenfranchised urban youth are viewed and treated within the school system move both teachers and students toward a new path? At WRS, the staff built a program based on students' expressed needs. They also continuously mould and shape their practice in order to meet ongoing and changing demands. In this inner-city environment, teachers have found it necessary to ensure that all their meetings with youth, and especially the first ones, sew the seeds for positive school experiences. Staff are welcoming and accepting; they try to foster a sense of belonging in their students. Their goal is to provide emancipatory education by paying close attention to the needs of their students. Teachers and youth workers understand that relationships are crucial in a school environment where everyone is encouraged to be critical and open.

CREATING THE CONDITIONS TO BREAK
THE STATUS QUO

WHEN I SPOKE WITH senior staff members at WRS about how they encourage critical thinking and critical teaching at the school, the first thing they emphasized was that early communications between teachers, youth workers, and students need to be limited to frequent affirmative interactions. As James said, "I think that when they come in and there's a lot of support staff, they develop unique rapports with all of us. And then come to expect it when they come in the door. And it's that familiarity. I think it helps a lot, keeps them coming back...to see the same person, the same place, it just feels comfortable. I think that's a motivating factor in attendance."

It is essential that youth understand that they are accepted as individuals at WRS. Students need to know that it is okay to be who they are and that they are welcome in the place. As youth worker Leonard pointed out, "The school welcomes people, and I've heard students say that all the other schools had kicked me out except this one."

Yes, many students are just at WRS by default, but this tells us something important. In many cases, no one else would take them. These students, especially, need to know that WRS *will* take them and that it is a place that is warm and provides hot coffee and lunches. All of the senior teachers I spoke to couldn't emphasize enough how crucial comfort is in that first step in moving youth from the streets into formal education.

All the literature I've read about programs for disenfranchised urban youth agree that the schools work best when students feel safe, accepted, and cared for.[2] My experience at WRS supports this mandate, as well. I'll admit, at first, the program appeared to me to be lacking structure. It was messy, missing the formalities I was used to in other schools. Class changes were inefficient, noisy affairs. I thought that the whole thing begged improvement. However, the neat, mechanical structures of a public school would constitute a problem for youth who live lives characterized by lack of structure. And so, staff at WRS have focused attention on the importance of *lack* of structure. In the end, relationships are more important than structure.

When I asked the senior staff group about their first impressions and what youth would immediately notice about the environment in the school, many mentioned the sharing circles. Kristine explained the circles, which begin with everyone sitting on the floor in the gym. "We have circle three times a day. Basically it's to air problems, concerns; periodically, it becomes more administrative-based and so we're taking attendance. But a lot of times it'll be a student takes attendance. A student facilitates the circle and it's done on a weekly basis, and so each week in theory gets a different student and they take responsibility for the classes starting, the circle starting, and people going to class. And everyone has an equal voice in the circle." 111

An education that is effective for all students strives for equal participation of disenfranchised voices and legitimizing experiences in schools. Again, what came through to me most in my conversations about the circles was the importance of equal relationships at WRS. The structure of the circle fosters a particular type of relationship between students and those in positions of greater authority. Teachers and students both realize, of course, that there is an implicit hierarchy of power at school, and during "circle" teachers do look for certain behaviours or signs that have meaning only to the teacher. While the students have voice it is tempered by the power teachers hold to evaluate what students are saying. That said, WRS youth felt they were silenced in public schools through negative interactions with teachers and peers. Being able to speak up during "circle" goes a long way toward finding a sense of belonging in this school. When students feel they have a voice, they have power: an opportunity to contribute their knowledge to a greater whole and to change their realities.

It makes sense that programs that recognize knowledge as power are more effective for youth who have traditionally been marginalized in schools. But I wanted to find out directly from students how effective the circle was as a space for sharing power in the school. Students seemed to appreciate and see the value in circles. Kevin told me, "The circle...the students get a chance to voice their own opinion about how the school should be run or certain rules that should be done or not done." And virtually all the students I interviewed commented on the importance of being able to talk openly with staff and other students in a non-judgmental atmosphere. But how does a non-judgmental approach work at WRS? How does it help, and how does it hinder, students?

Thinking about the Non-judgmental Approach

As a teacher I, too, began to think that being non-judgmental was an important component in my relationships with students. With time, however, I also came to believe that I needed to contribute some of myself to the relationship. If students are to feel truly valued in a relationship, sharing of voices needs to be involved. When students share themselves and we as teachers respond appropriately we are only getting at one aspect of building a relationship. At first, I felt that sharing my middle-class life with them was inappropriate, as I have earlier noted. However, my students seemed to enjoy giving me, the middle-class mom, advice on which rock concerts I should and should not let my twelve-year-old son attend, what type of MP3 player is best for a child, and even how to avoid having my car broken into in the parking lot. While these topics may sound trivial and even inappropriate, they provide an opportunity for youth to share what they have to offer. I felt that I was being given a nod of approval when the youth who was an expert at stealing cars shared his knowledge with me. Maybe his knowledge was validated in that instance. Maybe I was validated by him, as being worthy of receiving that knowledge. Of course, validating his knowledge related to illegal activity raises other troubling questions, but as teachers we cannot effectively shape behaviours without first establishing relationships with youth. A critical approach to schooling and teacher-student relationships allows for dialogue about how a young person might get into such activities in the first place, creating an opportunity for youth to be critical about themselves and others. This kind of dialogue-based analysis allows youth to understand ways in which their behaviours reflect unfair structures in society, and how they entrench their place in the larger community. Change comes when they are involved in a dialectic process of reflection and action.

New teachers also understand the importance of providing students with an opportunity to talk openly. Talking about a student, Meg told me, "She just really craves the time to talk about anything. When she got kinda a feel that she could pretty much say whatever cause I don't care, like I'm pretty open...then when we started walking places for Phys Ed she'd start tellin' me all this stuff and I think that's probably why she comes, just to get some time with somebody that doesn't judge."

Meg's words revealed to me an important insight about the needs of WRS students. Knowing that this youth *needed* to talk about her life without prejudgment by teachers is somewhat incongruent with what some of the complaints had been about early service teachers at WRS. Meg had come to an awareness that WRS students needed something different than what her teacher training had prepared her for. I wondered if her ability to see this in her students came through staff meetings, other discussions, or by her experiences in the classroom.

Talking to Meg made me challenge my earlier understanding that teachers who aren't introduced at university to the ideas about teaching that abound at WRS are resistant to them. Does knowing that these youth require individualized care and attention create tension between what they know to be effective teaching practice in schools? It seems likely that new teachers need additional time to bring their pedagogical practices in line with student needs at WRS. I wondered: Were they to enjoy better pay, job security, benefits, and satisfactory working conditions (the absence of fluctuating room temperatures, poor lighting, building that isn't clean, mouse traps) would they stick around long enough to begin to absorb the practices promoted by more senior staff? Meg did indicate to me that job security would make a difference in her commitment to the school. "The staff here rotates quite frequently. I don't know if that's due to the situation or the unstableness...and that's the thing, it's not the job that I wouldn't come back to, it's the unstableness of whether next year there's going to be a whole year. And if I got offered a full-time stable job, then it would be, like now I have something that I can count on."

When I think about my own development as a teacher in this environment, I realize that some of my knowledge came from learning to listen and be guided by more experienced staff, especially those who had lived through difficult circumstances as young people. But a great deal of my teacher practice and instincts came from being actively engaged as a graduate student while I was a teacher. I believe that external, formal learning greatly helped me to teach at WRS, that and structured opportunities to reflect on personal practice. In-service training, for example, is important to teaching in general, but at WRS it needs to be more extensive. Teachers at schools like WRS need to be taught about concepts like critical pedagogy, popular theatre, poverty and education, and sociological understandings of race and gender. While informal learning—between senior teacher and new teacher—in this program is invaluable to teacher development, formal learning informs new teachers about (and validates) the practices present in the school.

Fostering a Sense of Belonging

I have noted that staff ensure that early meetings with youth at WRS are safe and welcoming and lay the groundwork for building respectful relationships. Slowly, as these relationships are extended and deepened, youth come to see the school as a place where they belong. They begin to take ownership of the school. For some it is like a home.

On a recent visit to the school, I spoke with Kristine, who, quite excitedly, talked about a group of students who had been in the school for about half a year. I knew some of them from my literacy class when they first arrived the previous winter. Their attendance was sporadic and engagement in class work was difficult. Most were coming off heavy drug use and had had recent contact with the law. To them, this school was, like other schools, worthy of resistance. Over the summer they came regularly to outreach, a recreational program at the school. Academic classes were not being offered, but they were still coming. Once September rolled around, one of the youth was reported to be wandering about the group home in the morning telling his friends to get up to go to school. Somehow ownership had evolved. Now, Kristine told me, their attendance was quite regular and they seemed committed to WRS. James explained:

> For most of the youth, their lives are so unstable that the school represents one of the stable factors in their lives and in many cases the only stable factor in their lives. It's a safe place that they can come to and escape a harsh environment. In the process, the shift that has to take place because we do our best to build community here, and many

times students come to see the community almost as a family and to replace the sense of family that they don't actually have in their own lives.

When James referred to "the shift that has to take place" he meant that there needs to be movement from those first meetings between staff and students that focus on positive interactions and encouraging comfort in the school to more in-depth relationships, wherein students start to see themselves as active members of the school community.

There are a number of problems that rear up from first meeting with students to seeing them begin taking ownership of WRS. It is difficult to focus on positive exchanges, for example, when those first meetings are also important for noting behaviours that help us teachers "code" and for conducting intake assessments with students. While James noted, "We try to keep the process respectful," it is difficult. A relationship built on sharing and respect cannot include "coding." Or can it? Maybe it's not so different from a teacher–student relationship that involves marking and assessment. But relationships in *this* school are intended to be different.

I spoke with some senior staff members about the ways in which they work around problems like coding in their relationships with students. Leonard said, "It's all built on trust. They have to learn to trust you first. So it's, I guess you could say, just witty bantering at first. Just small conversations here and there, probing with the right questions and then eventually they find I'm more of a friend. They know they can talk to me about anything, but it takes time you know, there's something I have to work on with them is gaining their trust."

James elaborated by saying, "There's still problems, because, cooperation and respect, it's a process and they're all going through it... And I think sometimes we have to keep reminding ourselves that we need to go through it as well." Leonard and James seemed to believe that, as with all relationships, WRS relationships also take effort, but the effort is often intense and rewards are often not immediately apparent.

Many WRS students have received very little trust and love and may need more time to develop positive relationships. I found, sometimes, that I had to take some abuse before cracking the shell, and that can be difficult for teachers and youth workers. For this reason, staff must be empathetic toward the youth in order to maintain their desire to keep working at building difficult relationships. The reward comes later when they begin to see their students developing a sense of belonging and an increased self-esteem. Hence, the excitement in Kristine's voice when she was telling me about the group of students who had finally begun to feel that WRS was their school, their place.

A number of the students I spoke to about relationships at WRS talked about the social structure of the school as an important component contributing to a positive environment. Sara told me, "It's more the people here, they act really comfortable here. I know everybody's name, everybody knows my name and we can all say hi to each other and the teachers, I like the fact that...call them by their first name and talk to them about whatever...like it's been good for me, like self-esteem wise and everything like that, because I don't think anybody really hates... everybody just tries to respect each other and it's all about, like um... good people here."

I also found out that once students have discovered that WRS is a place where they *can* belong and where they *want* to belong, many will stand up for it when they feel it is threatened. Leonard recalled a particular student, then the general student body, when illustrating this fact to me: "She has a loyalty to the school, a lot of students here are like that, like they say, 'I don't care what anyone thinks. If something's going wrong, I'm going to tell somebody because I don't want it to take place in my school.'"

Successful programs for students who have left mainstream schools are ones that students feel ownership for. I wondered if WRS students felt ownership for their school because they felt personally validated and comfortable, or perhaps because they understood the school in broader terms. Did they understand WRS as a place where youth *like them* who are "at-risk," coded, or "special needs," are validated?

As a teacher at WRS I also observed ownership behaviour. One day during circle, a student urgently expressed a desire to discuss a concern that she had. Somehow circle ended without the concern being addressed. She pressed the issue further, and circle was reconvened. She complained that another student had been seen doing "jib" in the girl's washroom. She accused the teachers of ignoring the problem and was quite sure we were all aware that it was going on. I sat very quietly hoping I wouldn't have to admit that I didn't even know what "jib" was. I later found out that it is "speed," in the language I understand, and you would know someone is using it by the way his or her eyes looked, darting around continuously. The problem with this behaviour from the perspective of the student who brought it up is that it puts the school in jeopardy.

WRS is funded by a variety of sources both public and community. Representatives of funding bodies would not appreciate funding a school for current drug users, and students do not want behaviours such as this to put the school's funding at risk. If the school were to close, many of these youth would have difficulty finding other places in which to complete their schooling. As James pointed out, "Many of them [students] see this as their last chance to get an education. I think most of the students who come to the school sincerely would want to get an education, want to complete high school, but the realities of their early socialization and day to day environment make it challenging to say the least."

These are youth who see the value in a high-school diploma and are aware that formal education is an important component in future successes. Many see WRS as the only possible avenue to achieve that goal, a contributing factor in their sense of ownership of the school.

Encouraging "Success"

Alongside cultivating a sense of belonging in students, teachers also engage students in a series of steps toward academic definitions of success. The eventual goal is high-school completion and an academic diploma. Some students struggle through these academic stream courses and have the option of completing a general degree, but ultimately WRS is a high-school program that aspires to have students achieve the formal education needed for access to workplace and further education. As James told me, "It is a long-term process. And that's one of the things that makes us different [as a school]. It's a long-term program. We have programs intended to bring people in off the streets, move them from the streets into the school, or into youth support program, from the youth support program into [WRS], from [WRS] to writing departmental exams and encouraging them to look at post-secondary. And they're all different steps, and it's a long route."

The WRS process takes many years, with most students venturing into it quite slowly. As mentioned earlier, many students stop and start a number of times before completing the initial literacy courses. Once they develop a routine of coming to school regularly, there is still a long-term commitment needed to reach high-school completion, as many need additional courses to fill in gaps in academic skills.

Initially students' successes are defined in a variety of academic and non-academic ways, as are reflected in the following comment by James. "For some students, just coming to school on a regular basis is success. And we let them know that, as well. Coming to school on time is success. Not fighting in school—success. You know, even if they just come here for one or two terms and then have a different way of looking at the world, are able to co-operate with each other, that's success. And then they move onto other programs and that's just fine. And that happens as well."

Unfortunately, it is difficult to find books or articles that discuss redefining measures of success for disenfranchised urban youth. In 2001, Alberta Learning acknowledged the importance of listening to and supporting disenfranchised students who are dealing with complex problems in their lives.[3] However, it did not recognize the importance of greater flexibility in areas such as attendance and coming to school on time, or providing additional funding to schools like WRS, which teach such students. Success in Alberta learning institutions is ultimately about high-school completion and results on diploma exams. And this kind of "success" is familiar to us. We live in a society defined by success as measured by academic achievement, status through employment, and the accumulation of material things. People who have these *things* are considered successful. With Alberta Learning still focusing on this type of success, public schools continue to avoid examining "process" as a way to gauge the "progress" of disenfranchised youth.

I have occasionally been involved in academic discussions regarding alternate definitions of success, but these are generally not focused on making concrete changes in schools. While a school like WRS is built on and understands different ways of looking at success, how do WRS *students* define success? Would they see themselves as successful when they are able to get themselves to school on time, or are they still a product of a society that defines success in ways not readily accessible to them? Senior staff challenge and reshape students' perceptions about "success," but what about that troubling coding process that says something different in terms of success? If success is defined by the requirements of "special needs" funding as the absence of swearing, and an accurate portrayal of street life in drama, or writing, or video requires swearing, students must see the contradiction. What it comes down to is that WRS teachers need to initially validate students' lived experiences before encouraging them to both challenge and understand the norms of middle-class behaviour and values, such as the concept of "success."

When I spoke with senior staff, they offered additional ideas about success when they talked about WRS's drama program. Claire said, "I think just participating...being there, talking, adding to something. Doing a game when you haven't done it before. You can choose to participate...and for some to just do 'what are you doing' or something like that, which is where you're actually put on the spot."

Kristine added, "Measures of success can be really small." These small, incremental degrees of success happen in drama and literacy programs, which help students become part of the school community. Popular theatre has played an integral role throughout the history of WRS; it was, after all, the practice out of which the school itself evolved.

POPULAR THEATRE AND MEDIA AT WRS

AT TIMES POPULAR THEATRE is woven into WRS's programming, at other times it is limited to an extracurricular drama group that meets independently within the school once per week. That is, not as a formal element within the classroom but as a group of interested participants working toward a variety of performances that usually take place outside the school. Early drama experiences include games and popular theatre exercises to enhance student participation and feelings of comfort in the school. Kristine told me about one of these games and what students think about them.

> We have a young guy who has been meeting in drama every week since last summer, and I don't know if it was this week or the week before this...we did a game where you have to mime in the middle of the circle and he participated in it and it's the first time in a year. Most people arrive at that point a little sooner but [arriving at a point of comfort] is very personal. And he had other successes. He's actually been on a stage in front of an audience. But he actually put himself on that line [mime game] because someone else decides what you're going to do so you really have to trust the people you're playing with and you're very much not in control. And so to allow yourself not to be in control that way is...to give up the power.

Being comfortable and trusting one's fellow actors is an essential precursor to popular theatre participation.

WRS's popular theatre is reminiscent of a similar program in Brazil, written about by an educator named Augusto Boal. The program Boal writes about has the mission of eradicating illiteracy. Boal says that students need to be comfortable participating, and they also need to develop knowledge, control, and expressiveness of their bodies.[4] If they do this, participants can take on the role of actors: ceasing to be objects and becoming subjects. Boal points out that initial contact with a group can be difficult because the educator comes with the mission of eradicating illiteracy, which youth could see as coercive. For this reason, he suggests that the theatrical experience should begin with something familiar to the people, such as, the bodies of those who agree to participate. A focus on bodies leads into a number of drama exercises designed to promote awareness of one's own body and ways to interpret and make expressive the portrayals of others.

In the WRS situation, students also arrive with feelings of apprehension toward educators who have traditionally played coercive roles in their lives. Youth's earlier school experiences provide reason for creating conditions of community before jumping in to creating theatre about the social conditions of participants. Tim Prentki and Jan Selman, educators discussing the potential for social transformation, define popular theatre as a *process* that encourages communities to identify their concerns, analyze current conditions and causes of a situation, see points of change, and figure out how change could happen.[5] Prentki and Selman also suggest that popular theatre can help participants work on "dangerous issues…clarify their views, to investigate dilemmas, to analyze their social, political and economic situations, to challenge assumptions, to strategise, to 'rehearse for action,' and to share their insights with others within and without their immediate community."[6]

The notion of "dangerous issues" interests me. What is a dangerous issue? Is it one that could explode in your face? Probably, but that's part of a critical process. What's more important at WRS is limiting the danger for youth, only opening wounds within a process of healing. So how do we do that? Some might argue it is better to leave these issues alone. It would be more comfortable for youth in the short term to let sleeping dogs lie. But long-term, sustained comfort requires an empowerment to act upon one's world.

Certainly the issues youth and staff members at WRS are exploring through popular theatre can be painful ones. Youth need to identify the topics and experiences they wish to explore and be actively involved in developing their own approaches to the issues. Popular theatre allows this to happen.

James, a senior teacher, told me, "Since popular theatre exercises are most often about social issues, then the kind of analysis that takes place is fairly significant, as well. It often takes place just through presenting scenes without any kind of moralizing by the facilitators and it's the youth or students [who] are able to draw what they're ready for from that process."

In this process, students join their awareness of reality with a program of action. Teachers, or facilitators, as members of the popular theatre community, recognize their roles are not neutral. My own understanding of issues of importance to youth was altered by involvement in popular theatre exercises with them. They often identify police brutality as an issue and create a dramatic image that is very different from those we see in the media. Through popular theatre I have seen real people as the victims of police brutality, not the nameless, faceless criminals in mainstream media who don't require us to examine both sides of the issue. Why does a young man need to have his face slammed into the side of his car in order to be arrested, when he is unarmed? Why does a young woman need to be ridiculed because she is addicted to drugs and homeless?

All of these same issues come up in literacy courses, as well, where comfort and trust also need to be precursors. Leonard talked with me about the literacy courses. "A lot of the kids that have come here haven't experienced any kind of success, be it through a job or anything. I've heard stories where people have been stuck working in bottle depots counting bottles, and that's where they saw themselves, as just being there. Then they come here and they complete two or three credits and they're beaming."

Richard told me that it isn't just the completion of courses that fosters success but also the arts-based focus within these courses. "The digital media...I think the number one success for sure is the confidence in one's abilities that they get from producing artwork so rapidly, and it's so visible. But there's also, I think, an incidental learning almost, where they learn a variety of computer skills and they become familiar with various applications and they can generalize to other digital media applications more readily."

Photography is also prominent in these courses. The students take cameras and head out to photograph their world; teachers let them tell their own stories. Photography becomes a language, a way to answer questions about one's life. Very simple questions—such as "Where do you live?"—can lead to very powerful images and themes that the group develops together. James said, "I think they learn a lot about their own environment, their own social situation, and I think they learn a lot about choices to make, to overcome some of those issues that they've previously maybe been overcome by."

Socially conscious students are willing to discuss the choices they have made, often leading to involvement with the law, and the choices that are there for them to make once they have the understanding and confidence needed in order to exercise them. When youth first arrive at the school many have an appreciation of some of their own behaviours as "bad" choices and have self-images that correlate. But when they come through the literacy and popular theatre programs, they become aware of a social world that enabled them to make "bad" decisions, and they also become aware that they can make better choices for themselves personally and for their environment.

The character Slash and his life story, in the book *Slash* by BC Aboriginal writer Jeanette Armstrong, embodies the course of action that happens at WRS. Difficulties growing up in a traditional home in an Aboriginal community on a reserve while attending a predominantly white school in town, where he experienced racial taunts and social exclusion, leaves Slash confused about his place in the world and angry with white people and structures of mainstream government. Armstrong paints a haunting portrait of the frustrations, sense of inadequacy, and hopelessness felt by many Aboriginal youth who share similar life circumstances and experiences.

123

Readers can feel Slash's pain, but they also see how Slash makes things worse for himself and his people by blindly following his path. In the end, although he recognizes there were barriers up against him in school and in the workplace, Slash also comes to realize that he does have choices outside the drug trade.

> It felt good to be with just Indians, young ones, who were seriously attacking a problem only they seemed to understand. One which I understood better and better. I finally understand why I had deserved to be punished for working in the dope business. The Johnny Johns and the people who helped them just helped our people into the gutter.[7]

Staff members at WRS demonstrate they are wise to Slash's realizations, as Leonard explained to me. "Life is filled with choices. It's like, you're the writer, you write it. It's not written out for you and you have to follow the script to a T. You write it. You're the writer of your own life. And you decide which way you want it to go. I tell them this all the time. Some of them still don't believe me and they think, 'I'm scum, I'm going to stay scum, I was born scum and I'm going to die scum.'"

Making decisions to effect changes in one's life is wrought with difficulties when so many barriers need to be overcome, including beliefs that reinforce the existing social order through voluntary consent. Confidence comes from the power to act and change one's surroundings.

I have made choices informed by the power to act, but where does that power come from and how did I know when I had it? How many "bad" choices did I make before coming to understand I had the power to make "good" choices? For me, as a teenager, it was all about having the self-confidence to say no to things I didn't want to do but went along with because that's what the group was doing. Growing up with emotional abuse quickly strips away positive feelings of self-worth and the associated power to take risks and make informed decisions. Growing up with an alcoholic parent, as I did, and as many of the youth did, also means seeing excessive drinking as "normal" and therefore not a bad choice.

How will students know when they have the power to act? Is it partly dependent on developing a sense of what a good choice is? Will they have the confidence and desire to use their power to make these decisions? Often they need to resist what they know and are comfortable with in order to affect change. In the process of developing self-confidence, youth will glean knowledge that will implicate people they care about. For example, if drug use is deemed to be a bad thing, how do youth reconcile a parent's drug use? Are we addressing the problem of conflicting messages between home and school?

For myself, I have learned from my experiences at WRS that I make choices, and I write my own life with them. In terms of this book, for example, I have wondered whether I am using my power to act to facilitate change in Edmonton's inner city or whether I am just hiding away writing about it because it is more comfortable. While writing helps me clarify the power that I hold, what I do with that power to affect change in the future will require a commitment to choices that transfer that power.

CRITICAL LITERACY IN HIGHER-LEVEL CLASSES AND THE EXAMPLE ISSUE OF POLICE BRUTALITY

As STUDENTS BECOME AWARE of their environment they also become ready to move to higher-level courses and more academic definitions of success. As James said, "that element of exams and completing courses is there." Senior WRS teachers always intend—although this intention isn't always realized—to continue encouraging students to be critical of their world throughout their school experience in order to broaden and deepen their power to act within their communities. Yet this critical approach is not apparent in many upper-level courses, particularly courses taught by newer teachers who don't seem to recognize the need to continue with critical discussions. As Meg said, "when you've made it to the thirty levels [courses] you should be ready for school." Meg notes that students believe this, too. When discussing the need to prepare students for higher-level courses, she noted they only want to take courses that lead to graduation, "only stuff that'll get you done." Both students and new teachers need greater awareness of, not only the ways, but also the need for, incorporating critical discussions into academic courses.

Ultimately we have to move students toward being critical of their environment, and this requires them to seriously evaluate their experiences. This includes their experiences of being labelled, and how those judgments made about them, by teachers and other authority figures, informs how they view themselves. As mentioned above, we also need to consider the ways a critical approach can be better incorporated into higher-level academic courses. When teachers talk about this approach at WRS, they call it critical literacy. Ira Shor, a professor at the City University of New York Graduate School and leader in the field of critical literacy, provides a definition:

We are what we say and do. The ways we speak and are spoken to help shape us into the people we become. Through speech and other actions, we build ourselves in a world that is building us. We can remake ourselves and society, if we choose, through alternative words and dissident projects. This is where critical literacy begins—words that question a world not yet finished or humane.[8]

As we can see, though, simply "choosing" alternative words and dissonant projects is not as straightforward as it might seem for WRS students and their teachers. One challenge for teachers is to find time in the classroom to work with issues deeply while meeting the demands of a rigorous curriculum. My experience with teaching social studies at WRS is that a multitude of resources existed that would expand the topics under discussion, but I had to carefully choose which aspects of the curriculum I wished to enrich because of time limitations. I made these decisions based on my own beliefs about what was important. I needed to recognize that I had the power to make those decisions.

Instruction cannot be separated from the politics of literacy, and of labelling. I am constantly brought back to the student labelled through the coding process with literacy skills of "early elementary" yet holding knowledge and ability to use words such as "redemption" and "adversity." Within this context, the ways in which we make choices to remake ourselves and society seems like a bit of an uphill battle.

I have discussed the ways in which WRS teachers incorporate a variety of themes into literacy courses and how these themes often come out of drama exercises. The themes provide an "in" to opening up a conversation with youth and a way to begin working on reading, writing, and analytical skills. As students become more comfortable in the school, enhance their literacy skills, and move toward higher-level courses, we as teachers need to continue to be concerned with the issues. Taking police brutality as an example, having students write about their experiences serves the purpose of establishing a topic about which they have an opinion they can express in relation to themselves personally. Moving this topic into higher-level analysis means looking at the underlying issues of police brutality in the context of our lives. What are the historical relations between police and Aboriginal peoples in Canada? What is the history of youth justice in Canada? These and other questions begin the process of analysis of this issue.

For example, most Canadians believe—mainly as a result of information learned in schools—in the proud tradition of the Royal Canadian

Mounted Police. We then extend this belief toward other police services, such as the Edmonton Police Service. They are the *good* guys. If they are beating up on young people then the young people must be *bad* guys. We need to begin questioning these assumptions and historical understandings. This could prove to be a difficult task given a lack of available literature that might paint an alternative picture. As teachers, though, we can encourage other ways of viewing the world, other perspectives on historical topics and relations.

To continue with the police example, we can begin to liberate ourselves and our students by understanding what has been and how that informs our knowledge of the here and now. We can encourage students to look at how police treat people by considering gender, race, social class, and sexual orientation. We could also talk about issues such as the disciplinary action taken, in early 2005, against members of the Edmonton Police Service for circulating racist "jokes" that included slanderous comments about Aboriginal people. Do Aboriginal youth feel they would receive protection from police who harbour such feelings? How about gay and lesbian youth? Do these youth see police taking a stand against incidents of violence where gay or lesbian youth are victims?

Students at WRS occupy dislocated positions in relation to those who hold the power to define police actions. Their position outside the mainstream gives them a vantage point from which to question their relationship to it, in this case the police. Why do we unquestioningly obey laws that are not applied equally? Why do we allow discriminatory practices against those who occupy positions on the margins? How do abusive practices serve to prevent self-awareness in those who are abused? The story of disenfranchised urban youth, told in relation to mainstream policing practices, creates a disruption in the status quo. It gives all of us, students, teachers, and staff, a point of pause and a chance to reflect on the knowledge we have taken for granted.

Texts that provide starting points for analyses of this issue include *Slash* by Jeanette Armstrong, also mentioned above. The novel questions police brutality in relation to Aboriginal youth. Here Slash reflects on his experience in jail:

Some of them pigs liked to call you dirty racist stuff and did stuff to make you mad. One of them did that to me first-off when I got there. It was during a line-up to go out in the yard. We had to pass through this screen gate, one at a time. This pig stood right beside it and roll called as we went through. When I came up, he stuck his foot out and would have tripped me but I was still strong enough to twist and catch my balance before his foot hooked me. His knee came up and caught me in the balls as he said, "Don't ever try and screw with me, Geronimo, or you'll understand what scalping means."[9]

Given earlier discussions with WRS youth regarding their own personal experiences with police, teachers can use this passage from *Slash* as a springboard into analysis of historical relations between police and Aboriginal peoples and how they continue to be played out in Canadian prisons. How does this passage make students feel? How does this passage make teachers feel? Feelings of anger, frustration, and helplessness show just how far apart the mainstream belief in police fairness and the realities of young people's lived experience really are.

In Canada we are progressive. We assume innocence until guilt is proven. So why have many WRS students experienced police brutality while being arrested? I wouldn't expect that treatment from police, so why do these youth expect it? Maybe because I am white and middle class and they are disenfranchised through poverty, abuse, and skin colour. They know they have no voice to complain about their treatment. It will just result in more abuse. In my case, I have power to complain if I am mistreated. I can mobilize resources including money, people in positions of power, and public opinion. If I were to be a victim of police brutality the public would be outraged, the media would have a field day. Does the power that I hold keep police from harassing me? I suspect they don't hold any animosity toward me anyway. Why would they? I don't break any laws. I'm a law-abiding citizen. I pay my taxes and contribute to the economy.

Discussions that begin with teachers saying such things can heighten overt awareness of the issues at play within young people's experiences of police brutality. Teachers can add layers to the analysis by adding other books to the discussion. *Runaway: Diary of a Street Kid*, by Evelyn Lau, is one such book. Here is Lau's experience with youth detention:

> *We arrived at detention—a flat, solid brick building. The snickering cop assured me it would be just like a motel, except I'd be locked in. A swarm of flies attacked us in the hall before we entered another door, where a woman seated me in the admittance room and asked me a list of questions, mostly medical things. In another room they were having a debate about whether detention could legally hold me, but this question was cleared up when one policeman conveniently announced that I could be lying and they should keep me until my parents could be tracked down.*[10]

How does this passage make students feel? She was "snickered" at by the police. Not really the same thing as being "kicked in the balls." Lau is being treated as a runaway, a girl who is being naughty. She needs to be returned to her Chinese, middle-class parents. She is not being taken seriously and is clearly frustrated throughout her time on the streets by this aspect of her experience. Using this text in class, I have found many WRS students react similarly to her plight. They don't understand the "abuse" she claims at the hands of her middle-class parents who seem to simply want her to work hard and do well. It doesn't compare to their personal experiences of abuse. So are Lau's claims of abuse real? They resonated with me as I read her diary. I felt the loveless home, the unhappiness, and the strain of hiding in her bedroom hoping to not be noticed.

Lau's book has allowed me to add social class and other factors to the analysis of police brutality. In what ways can "abuse" be experienced differently? How do we reconcile *degrees* of abuse? Is *any* level of abuse acceptable? What is the difference between a "runaway" and a youth who is "street involved?" Is a runaway simply a middle-class youth who is being naughty, while a "street kid" is disenfranchised, urban, poor, and breaking the law. The power of language works to name experiences in particular ways that benefit some and further marginalize others. Who holds this power? Questioning power structures offer ways to take our knowledge apart and allow students' experiences to speak about them instead. But we can't just leave it at that. We also need to reassemble, to build theories of political action. We need to move beyond binaries of social class, race, and gender, and raise central questions about the power to act. If we want to empower students to change police brutality we have to see and teach its complexity.

I also believe that teachers need to bring examples of community action for social change into the curriculum. For example, in 2000, Stephen Brown, an educator who spent time teaching in Alaska, wrote about bringing into his Athabascan reserve classroom the conflicts between the reserve subculture and the dominant Euro-American culture. He talked mostly about environmental issues, and through that both teacher and students saw power relations laid bare. Providing a forum in the classroom for students to speak and write on the issues of today increases the chances they will become spokespersons for their communities tomorrow. Without knowledge of the vocabulary used by those in positions of power it is difficult to enter the dialogue. Teaching students to be critical is about the transference of power. It is about learning the language that allows you to claim the power to rename your world. It is about creating opportunities in the classroom for this to happen.

THERE ARE MANY WAYS we can challenge how disenfranchised youth are viewed and treated in schools. The important thing is to recognize knowledge as power when we look to resources to help us reshape youth from objects into subjects. A critical literacy joins this awareness of power with a program of action that enables students to take control of their lives. What is revealed by this particular story, of WRS, is a process, a path that can be followed and talked about by those educators looking for alternative ways to educate disenfranchised youth.

SIX   CONCLUSIONS: THE STORY SPEAKS

Knowledge of self is more like ignorance than knowledge. The more deeply I go, the less clear my self-knowledge becomes, the more ambiguities and perplexities and unresolved contradictions I discover.[1]

WATCHING THE "ROSES" at WRS reach upward, and writing about their growth, and the way in which the WRS community helped stimulate that growth, was an uplifting process for me that revealed so much about possibilities for urban youth in all schools. WRS's pedagogical processes make clear to both alternative and mainstream schools the importance of employing different approaches for disenfranchised urban youth. By researching, talking to staff and students, reading outside sources, and teaching in the classroom, I became critically aware of middle-class assumptions and beliefs about young people, schooling, and society.

Of course, what this book offers you, the reader, is simply one moment in time. Schools are constantly evolving systems operating in complex environments. However, what I hope I've offered here are new paths that other schools might wish to tread, and new ways for people to talk about education. I also hope I've revealed something to WRS and other schools like it, which are constantly looking for better ways to engage youth whose needs are currently not met by the public-school system.

THE PROCESS OF DISCOVERY

MY RESEARCH WITH WRS was an organic thing, and it would not have worked well if I had tried inserting data into a ready-made framework. The research had to be allowed to grow into and speak for itself. I discovered that process was just as important for this book as it was for the students and staff I was speaking with. Unlike the research I have worked on for other projects, I found that the phases of research for this project were somewhat arbitrary. There was no clear dividing line that marked the end of my data collection, the beginning of my analysis, and the writing up of my findings. The act of writing also became part of the discovery, data collection, and analysis phases. Also unlike other projects, I have a personal stake in this one. The final product speaks from who I am in the research, and others would surely offer a different perspective. However, rather than a detriment, I believe this personal element, this "voice" is important. As teachers and researchers, our voices reveal something important. I think this mirrors what I found to be essential in my research on WRS: the voices.

In addition, my understanding of my research evolved out of engaging in teaching at WRS. I did not enter into this project with a clear idea of where I was going, rather, my path emerged through critical pursuit. Significantly, my decision to include my voice in this research, almost like a conversation with myself, demonstrates how important teacher self-discovery is in the process of finding new pedagogical paths. Because I was both immersed in WRS and literature about similar programs, I feel I made informed decisions about how to tell the story. Thus, it became a story about "us" not "them." Knowing this gave me the security to speak freely, especially where my recordings of events may have cast teachers and/or youth workers in a negative light. Understanding that my own practices reflected much of what they were doing made the writing down of everything more comfortable for me. I think this process allowed me to take responsibility for changing myself.

The story, as it is written in this book, was co-created in the weaving together of voices. By following a critical process, I found I could merge my prior experiences with the words of WRS participants and of others, whose words I found rang true.

Of course, this whole process was somewhat messy! Certainly the idea of messiness makes it difficult to establish whether one has engaged in research effectively. Still, while there are no clearly defined boundaries to my inquiry about WRS, I did rely on informed judgments to guide the way. I required myself to underpin the whole process with a deep attentiveness to language and what words point to historically. Of course, I didn't intend to rewrite history, but how can we speak about events in the here and now when historical facts are so disputed? I think that I could have achieved an even deeper understand of WRS and its position if I had been able to engage in more conversations with research participants regarding their personal and family histories and the ways in which they derive historical meaning.

Another requirement I had for myself in the process of this inquiry was to take personal ownership of the project and be critical of how I interpreted details. It was an ongoing struggle to figure out how I have been influenced by the structures to which I am inextricably linked, such as my social and economic class, and my family history. I believe this story of WRS demonstrates the importance of both teachers and youth taking part in personal and social analysis. Engagement in a critical process with youth has helped me as educator to develop awareness of my own position in relation to an inner-city school and the ways in which my own power and privilege impact on my relationships both within and outside the school. WRS is a unique place where I was able to have multiple conversations in a special approach to teaching a high-needs group of students. I found out that new and different relationships brought new elements to the larger discussion I had, and still have, with a variety of people about meeting the needs of students who are currently experiencing difficulties in public school environments.

There are many layers to the analysis in this book, one of which points to the complexity of social divisions. Here, these social divisions include class, race, and gender. This list is not meant to be exhaustive but it is rather representative of current literature on disenfranchised urban youth. The ways in which we can interpret a group of people are limited only by our imaginations or by our lack of dialogue with others. As I have discovered, careful interpretation of social divisions is a creative process that involves understanding individuals and their differences. It is learning to highlight the interconnectedness of various elements within our own lives and discovering that the dominant ways of viewing the world are not simply common sense.

The roses tended so carefully at WRS so that they might bloom in self-discovery prompted self-discovery in me. While I was talking to youth and staff and trying to document the uniqueness and strengths of WRS, I found myself wondering: How do I know if I am *doing* the research properly and have made sense of my place in the research? My self-doubt allowed for a realization that my role as researcher was to demonstrate understanding of WRS from within, to find myself in the middle of stories, and to represent those stories in a multidimensional fashion. I knew I had to take up the task.

Taking up the task implies we are creating meaning, not simply reporting it. Engagement required me to know that I could not give an account of other people's thoughts and actions from their point of view. I knew I could only interpret what others told me by making use of our common language and experiences. Whatever I say about WRS students and staff I am also saying about myself. By carefully attending to all of us, I gained a deeper understanding of myself and the processes of teaching and learning at WRS. Because of this, I feel I have gained a richer vision of the lives of disenfranchised urban youth and those who struggle to ensure their place in a community that would otherwise exclude them. The resulting story illuminates a group of people who need to be noticed, not just for their own sake, but for all of us. Their story informs a missing piece of the educational puzzle, a piece many of us are struggling to find.

Whether or not I have told the story the way you might have, I have put the story out there so we can all begin to talk to each other. We can begin to talk about what works and what doesn't in terms of schooling practices for disenfranchised urban youth. We can talk about ways we can engage with youth as people, not objects, within an educational system that is bent on objectifying, by beginning to validate students' knowledge and experience. We can refocus on the processes of education with attention to ensuring the preconditions for learning are taken care of. And we can begin to talk about the need to raise the profile of schools that are struggling to meet the needs of disenfranchised urban youth in order to ensure that adequate funding is in place and teachers' needs for adequate working conditions are met. Additionally, I hope the interpretive framework that this book offers will provide a process for school-based researchers to enrich their knowledge about other ways of researching disenfranchised urban youth in schools.

135

WHAT THE WRS MODEL HAS TO OFFER

THIS STORY BEGINS WITH an understanding that accommodations have to be made in order to bring some students to a space where formal learning can occur. Over the course of writing this book, my knowledge of this path to learning evolved in part due to involvement in two significant events. The first was the co-authoring and presenting of a paper on WRS at a National Mental Health conference. The paper was co-authored with one of the youth workers at WRS and was on the topic of special needs funding. The discussions I had about this paper, during its writing and after its delivery, helped me to have ongoing involvement with disenfranchised urban youth that is integral to building trust and moving toward goals of academic success. The second event was a critical pedagogy symposium held at WRS in November 2005 that featured Ira Shor working with school staff, students, and members of the university and community. I was able to talk to Ira Shor, who talked about this same process of accommodations as creating the conditions for pedagogy, conditions that need to be attended to before specific learning methods can be employed in the classroom.

To accommodate is to adapt, and while there are adaptations being made at WRS, this notion does not get at the complexity of the underlying issues. If teachers are creating the conditions for a specific teaching–learning method, teachers and students need to find accommodation, comfort, before classroom learning can occur. However, I do believe that teaching–learning does occur at WRS even as accommodations are being made, even in the earliest stages of the program, in part because of the WRS focus on flexibility.

Early service teachers at WRS struggle to find a balance between flexibility, fairness, and meeting the requirements of the Alberta curriculum and student financing. In this teaching environment many chances need to be given when young people have so many struggles in their day-to-day lives. Attending school is often difficult for reasons ranging from lack of bus fare to being involved with the justice system. Without stable home lives these youth are not able to focus on or complete homework. At the same time, staff try to make sure youth are ready to move forward with their lives by the time they complete their high-school program. Post-secondary schooling and jobs require regular attendance; they require you to complete your work in a timely manner. Tension between the need to be flexible and the need to provide structure is apparent in daily teaching practice as teachers and youth workers try to weigh individual needs with larger group concerns. Learning to live with uncertainty, informed by self-examination of one's own values about classroom practice, seems to be what separates the early service teachers from the more experienced staff members on this issue. Part of this process for teachers involves realizing that poverty lays a variety of psychological pressures on youth, including exclusion. Living in poverty and feeling the rejection of others is particularly difficult for adolescents, who are only just starting to become self-aware.

My own process of understanding came about while teaching at WRS and doing graduate studies. I think many teachers often do not gain the knowledge they need to work in schools like WRS unless they become graduate students. Even WRS's emphasis on informal discussions about teaching was made much clearer for me in my graduate program. Senior staff members at WRS talked to me about new teachers' resistance to anything beyond what teacher training programs had taught them. It seems to me that teacher education programs need to take into account the needs of those students, which are not being met within the public system. For example, I do think that teacher training programs should be teaching the psychology of poverty informed by race and gender histories; critical and feminist approaches to teaching; and, action-based research within the classroom. While some of these topics are given a cursory treatment within teacher education programs, it is not enough. A much more integrated approach is necessary, including perhaps the modelling of alternative schools, highlighting examples like WRS.

Another important thing that teacher training programs would do well to incorporate in their curricula would be the meaning and practice of respect. The notion of respect has always been elusive. The word respect is thrown around a lot in discussions about educational practice, but what does it really mean? How do we measure and validate respect as an essential element of research and teaching? I have come to understand respect, through involvement with this school, as something that is felt. In what ways might "felt" respect help teachers in their classrooms and researchers in their projects? How do we know when people feel equality in the research process and in the classroom? The youth at WRS felt a distinct lack of respect, which contributed to them leaving school early. At WRS, where they began to find success in school, they felt respected. Teaching teachers how to have an empathetic approach that considers others' feelings of respect would go a long way toward helping youth stay in school.

Young peoples' ambitions are fuelled by how they fare in public schools. Disenfranchised urban youth feel that their futures are limited in relation to their peers, and they feel the material and social constraints of contemporary school and inner-city life. Over time, they come to blame these constraints on their own lack of effort. Still, they do not know about the historical, cultural, and contemporary schooling processes that serve to push them to the margins. Any power they hold to resist their own marginalization ends up expediting rather than hindering the process. At WRS, staff attempt to reshape young people's values to be more conducive to academic success, but in order to do so they must devalue the street knowledge the students have developed for survival. Initially the school's literacy program builds upon this street knowledge to help youth develop confidence and critical awareness. However, the attitudes and behaviours needed for long-term "traditional" academic success are very different from the knowledge disenfranchised urban youth possess. It is clearly necessary to value young people's experiences, just as it is important for WRS staff to encourage youth to value more traditional models even as they question that traditional knowledge that is currently so valued in public schools. A critical practice opens up possibilities for such questioning to occur.

The ongoing discussion about integrated versus segregated school programs for specific groups who are disenfranchised—who feel their voices aren't heard in public schools—also figures prominently here. Clearly there are many arguments to support a number of different approaches. I have found that the educational needs of disenfranchised urban Aboriginal youth can be met in integrated settings when educators focus on relationships built on respect and understanding. There is room for many initiatives and a variety of school practices. Certainly ongoing study into discovery of common elements that are working well, working marginally well, or not working at all would contribute significantly to educating such youth. As this book shows, disenfranchised urban youth, particularly Aboriginal youth who have had some experience in a variety of school contexts, need to be a part of continuing dialogue. Others need to be part of this discussion, as well, including teachers, youth workers, and Elders.

DISRUPTING THE STATUS QUO THROUGH UNCOMFORTABLE CONVERSATIONS

IN ORDER TO DISRUPT the status quo for the good of disenfranchised youth, we all must examine our assumptions via the continuing dialogue about educational practices I mention above. What we *know* to be true in the classroom, for example the need for a quiet, orderly environment, does not necessarily hold up in critical discussions. We need to converse with colleagues in order to add new perspectives to the way we think about teaching and the education system. More than that, we need to talk about things that might be uncomfortable, such as labelling, white privilege, gender roles, poverty, and abuse. After all, one can only understand others and their perspectives in relation to oneself, certainly not in advance of knowing them and talking to them.

The more we know about others and their experiences, the better able we as teachers will be to address the problems that disenfranchised youth face in school. For example, knowing that many disenfranchised urban youth in public school settings are not comfortable allows us to pursue ways of making them feel comfort, of finding a way to create comfortable spaces for them. Discomfort is not something to avoid talking about, but rather a topic that needs to be embraced. Only when youth find places of comfort are they in spaces where discomfort can be avoided. Such places may simply be where youth have found belonging, like at WRS. If educators talk about students being pushed to the margins, it can only help us to address issues of comfort and acceptance in mainstream schools. These are the places that are held in high regard: it is assumed that the best teaching jobs are in middle-class schools, the best education is gleaned from such schools, and the most prestigious journals about education are mainstream. Maybe we need to look for comfort in the margins. We need to challenge ourselves to embrace discomfort in order to achieve something better for schools.

It is also in conversations on and in the margins that we can find out how disenfranchised youth see themselves, how they have constructed their personas based on social class, gender, and race. These youth have built their desires, thoughts, and feelings—have built their self-images—as a result of being marginalized characters within public schools. This detrimental process contributes to them leaving those schools early. The youth I spoke with at WRS clearly understood their places in the margins through the ways in which they were treated and labelled by teachers and peers. Of course, the notion of middle-class white privilege must enter any dialogue about middle-class schools and labelling. As well, notions of gender are complex for these disenfranchised youth. However, while there are general differences in the experiences of disenfranchised males and females, all are affected by the conditions of their difficult social environments. For me, this story highlights my learning about research and teaching and its messiness. I firmly believe we need to embrace the complexities inherent in social divisions and take ownership of our place in our practices. In so doing, we can find ways to work with the tensions in schools.

TENSIONS OF PEDAGOGY REVEALED

THE TENSION INHERENT in educational programming at WRS should provide helpful hints for all educators. For example, the problem of labelling resides both at WRS and in the larger educational system. The labels, or codes, are important to WRS and other schools in terms of special needs funding, but at the same time, in public schools, labels allow teachers to rely on average, easily identified and applied treatments that reduce teachers' "need" to spend time and money on the complexity of the "coded" child. We need group labels in order to talk about certain groups of youth, but at the same time, these labels condemn youth to certain visions of themselves in relation to others at school.

I found that early service teachers at WRS believe that labels serve a productive purpose with disenfranchised youth. However, senior teachers and my own experience have taught me that the mainstream practice of labelling only serves to focus our attention on abstractions rather than individuals. In so doing, we fail to comprehend the realities of street life and the impact street experiences have on youth in public schools. In some respects we need labels, yet labels cause difficulties in their tendency to separate and exclude. A way around the tension between positive and negative aspects of labels is to recognize that any "identity" must be understood within the context of a given historical setting. "Identities" are always fluid.

Through time and engaged involvement with youth, WRS teachers and youth workers have developed a knowledge of disenfranchisement that has caused them to shift away from objectifying students through labelling and to move toward embracing each youth as an individual. These critical educators are continuously struggling to maintain hold of a vision of inclusive schooling that meets the personal needs of their students, while also conforming to the institutional requirements of education in Alberta. It is indeed a tightrope walk. Because of the constant tension at WRS, teacher education and ongoing in-service training plays an important role at the school.

Another problematic area for teachers and students at WRS lays in the way "success" is measured. Within this community, with WRS students having personal histories of exclusion and undeniable social and economic difficulties, success is measured slowly and incrementally. An important component of the process of "success" as demonstrated at WRS is the development of a critical literacy to challenge and include the voices of disenfranchised urban youth. The literacy practices at WRS have much to offer to discussions about schooling for disenfranchised urban youth. Literacy is a key consideration when addressing the needs of this population. "Successes" here are meaningful in all educational policies.

THE WRS MODEL AND ITS POTENTIAL CONTRIBUTIONS TO THE SOCIOLOGY OF EDUCATION

IT IS MY HOPE THAT this book will make voices heard that have not been heard before. WRS's ability to nurture roses in concrete gardens through its somewhat messy, tension-filled processes and attention to individual needs provides a model of a school that those engaging in educational sociology could learn much from.

Up until the 1970s, most educational sociologists focused on seeking objectivity through fact-like conclusions and generalizations about human behaviour and social interaction. However, they did not talk much about the *processes* of educating. They could tell us urban youth were falling through the cracks, but they could not elucidate approaches directed at solving the problem. Evidence-based, objective approaches have led us to seek all-encompassing answers to educational ills, but there is no one-size-fits-all approach that can be injected into schools from the outside.

A new sociology of education has been around since the 1970s and focuses on the processes of education.[2] Researchers in this wave of thinking have demonstrated the importance of interviews, focus-group discussions, and reflection on personal teaching practice. Those who participate in such research enter discussions as active subjects who are engaged in knowledge building. This type of interpretive research represents a turn in social science that questions the very foundations of the discipline. Without certainty, how can we inform? What we are searching for now are the bright spots that can illuminate an understanding that speaks through us about society and culture. Now, we learn about ourselves as contributors to the construction of a social world of which we are a part. Now, we learn about ourselves through interactions within a microcosm that then informs participation in a macro social world.

There have been significant changes in the life experiences of young people in industrialized societies in recent decades. However, I believe that life chances and experiences are still largely shaped by an individual's location within social structures.[3] However, these structures are becoming increasingly difficult to define as the power of the collective weakens and the values of the individual intensify. Structures like class, race, and gender work against young people's chances even while they come to regard the social world as unpredictable. The changing impact of these social structures on disenfranchised urban youth is highlighted by the experiences of WRS students.

Risks that arise within our unpredictable society are unequally distributed, with greater risks, such as not completing high school, adhering to those at the bottom of the ladder. While social inequality continues to exert a powerful hold over people's lives, it operates increasingly at the level of the individual rather than the group or class. People increasingly regard setbacks and crises as individual shortcomings with little recognition of societal processes outside of their control. The young people at WRS reflect this in blaming themselves for not finishing high school. They see themselves as lacking in relation to those in an educational system and labour market that does not allow them the same opportunities as those of other socioeconomic classes. At the same time, standardization in schools tends to blur integrated social class, racial, and gender differences by giving the impression of greater equality and opportunities for individual advancement without actually doing so. Standardized tests, for example, treat everyone the same, suggesting equality without an understanding that different starting points lead to different outcomes.

While gender and racial inequalities are coming to assume greater significance in our society, these social processes operate in increasingly complex ways for youth living in poverty. Andy Furlong and Fred

Cartmel, researchers at the University of Glasgow who look at young people and social change, argue collective identities have weakened.[4] For the purposes of this book and wrs, I would like to clarify that *traditional* collective identities have weakened. That is, for this group of youth, collective identity is no longer established along racial, neighbourhood, or social class lines. Rather collective identity is based on a community with a common experience of disenfranchisement. Within this community, young people develop allegiances in response to their involvement with the law, schools, abuse, poverty, and other factors. And these allegiances serve them in their struggle for survival in their risk-heavy environment.

Class positions may have weakened in the greater society, but choices are severely limited for those at the bottom. Under analysis, the illusion of equality in schools gives way to a clear picture of inequality, yet youth remain shaped by the messages they have internalized. Individuals are increasingly held accountable for their own fates, and this is true within schools, as well. Ironically, alongside this revolution of the individual, increasing competition for educational credentials and labour market opportunities mean that marginalized youth have even fewer opportunities in which to exert themselves as individuals.

Of course, within the disenfranchised youth community, individuals have had a variety of different experiences. For example, Aboriginal and non-Aboriginal youth have necessarily experienced different circumstances: historical, cultural, and personal.

I think we need to talk about differences, such as those between Aboriginal and non-Aboriginal students, in such a way that students and educators both recognize that their differences can unite them. At wrs, students do seem to have formed a common purpose, regardless of their differences. And educators at the school have united them as critical thinkers who want to make a difference in their own lives and in their communities. This is the "critical literacy" that I talk about in this book.

Within schools educators must develop a "*critical* literacy, *powerful* literacy, *political* literacy which enables the growth of genuine understanding and control of all of the spheres of social life in which we participate."[5] Literacy in this respect is not simply an economically driven skill, a continuum of learning that points an individual toward his or her goals; rather, it is a moral vision of knowledge and culture. Disenfranchised urban youth are leaving public schools with a low-level understanding of a body of knowledge that represents domination and exploitation by the mainstream practices that marginalized and excluded them.

Knowledge that is socially legitimate in schools is increasingly understood to reflect larger society. The emerging field of "urban literacy" has disenfranchised youth immersed in electronic media "texts" more than in traditional reading and writing activities. We know that urban youth are the highest users of electronic media (i.e. television, movies, video games), so it makes sense that these students could benefit from literacy studies that empower them to deconstruct dominant media narratives, develop critical media skills, and create their own counter-media narratives. The literacy program at WRS offers students the opportunity to examine social relations in an under-examined context—through electronic media.

At WRS, the critical literacy program offers effective ways for creating new texts (most often electronic media) and re-readings of existing texts. The ways in which teachers mediate and transform constructions of these texts is a crucial element of WRS's practice. WRS teachers' work with students in critical literacy should not only be helping students at this particular alternative school, it should also be informing teacher education programs regarding teaching students who experience difficult material and social realities.

As educational qualifications increasingly become the condition for legitimate access to jobs in the market place, particularly the dominant ones, the educational system tends increasingly to dispossess those who are lacking power and privilege.[6] As this book shows, the processes of school "choice" operate to provide the best chances to those who are capable of exercising those choices, while those who are disenfranchised are ultimately pushed out of mainstream schools. As was earlier noted, those who have real choice to access specialized programs, such as fine arts schools or sports academies, also have the financial and social means that enable them to prepare for and get into such programs.

A critical literacy, as a critique of power, struggles to disrupt this process of false "choice" but educators must constantly engage with students and other educators about the topic in order to counter it effectively. In addition to being unable to make "choices" in public school, schools have consistently represented disenfranchised youth in terms of what they lack. The youth at WRS told me about their desires for the material benefits an education can provide, yet they remained alienated from this possibility within public schools. A critical literacy can bring awareness to this discontinuity. Ultimately, a critical literacy moves beyond the type of schooling that leads to people acquiring power and material wealth to people who want to question what constitutes the public good.

All of this can be accomplished through active research (conversation with others) that pays close attention to language and its interpretation, through coming to know ourselves as teachers by interpreting our own teaching practices.

I arrived at my identity as a teacher at WRS through interactions with students and staff members. My active research offered me a way to ensure my critical practice avoids the trap of shaping the social order in a fixed direction. It also allowed me insight about the tensions inherent in pedagogical practice at WRS. At one point, I could see that I was complicit in maintaining social categories because of my position of power in the classroom. I felt a profoundly heightened ethical sense in my relationships with students when I was teaching disenfranchised urban youth who have been denied a place in mainstream schools. Without a sharing of "truths" between us there could have been no common shared reality, and thus no foundation from which to engage one another. This engagement is crucial to a critical teaching practice.

AT WRS EDUCATORS ACTIVELY engage in a process of understanding the educational experiences of a group of disenfranchised urban youth. My hope is that through this book, these understandings of youth will help other teachers and teacher educators to know disenfranchised urban youth differently, helping all of us to achieve greater successes in our classrooms. I also wish to extend these understandings to broader sociological discussions about research and schools in hopes they contribute to a more in-depth understanding of a group of young people who haven't been heard in sociology of education literature. Youth voices are vital to these understandings, as this book highlights. Ultimately, my hope is to lessen the struggles for schools like WRS, which engage in ongoing and genuine attempts to help youth move forward in their lives; and for the continued growth of the youth who have shown me that a rose *can* grow from concrete.

NOTES

PREFACE

1. Wild Rose Alternative School (WRS) is a pseudonym for the school that is the subject of this book.

INTRODUCTION

1. The voices of urban youth, youth workers, and teachers in this book are all given as pseudonyms to protect their privacy.

ONE

1. R. Ross, *Dancing with a Ghost* (Markham, ON: Octopus Publishing Group, 1991) xxiii.
2. D.G. Smith, "Hermeneutic Inquiry and the Pedagogic Text," in *Forms of Curriculum Inquiry* (Albany, NY: State University of New York Press, 1991), 193.
3. Stephen Brown, *Words in the Wilderness: Critical Literacy in the Borderlands*. (Albany, NY: State University of New York Press, 2000), 182.
4. Michael Eric Dyson, *Holler if you Hear me* (New York: Basic Civitas Books, 2001), 77.
5. Michael Eric Dyson, *Holler if you Hear me* (New York: Basic Civitas Books, 2001), 76.
6. Michael Eric Dyson, *Holler if you Hear me* (New York: Basic Civitas Books, 2001), 77.
7. P. Hoikkala, "Feminists or reformers? American Indian Women and Community in Phoenix, 1965–1980," in *American Indians and the Urban Experience* (Walnut Creek, CA: AltaMira Press, 2001), 127–46.
8. Kim Anderson, *A Recognition of Being: Reconstructing Native Womanhood* (Toronto, ON: Sumach Press, 2000), 36.
9. Michael Eric Dyson, *Holler if you Hear me* (New York: Basic Civitas Books, 2001), 77.

10. Alberta Learning, *Removing Barriers to High School Completion—Final Report*, Edmonton, AB, 2001.

11. Evelyn Lau, *Runaway: Diary of a Street Kid* (ON: HarperCollins Publishers Ltd., 1989), 209.

12. B. Mah, "Listen to the Children: They Don't Think They're Safe," *Edmonton Journal* (Edmonton), January 24, 2001, first edition.

13. A. Gamoran, "High Standards: A Strategy for Equalizing Opportunities to Learn?" in *A Notion at Risk* (New York: The Century Foundation, 2000), 99.

14. M. Lewis, "Interrupting Patriarchy: Politics, Resistance, and Transformation in the Feminist Classroom," in *Education is Politics: Critical Teaching Across Differences, Postsecondary* (Portsmouth, NH: Boynton/Cook Publishers, Inc., 2000), 104.

15. Rae Rosenthal, "Feminists in Action: How to Practice What we Teach," in *Education is Politics: Critical Teaching Across Differences, Postsecondary* (Portsmouth, NH: Boynton/Cook Publishers, Inc., 2000), 107–23.

16. Henry Giroux, *Teachers as Intellectuals: Towards a Critical Pedagogy of Learning* (Granby, MA: Bergin & Garvey, 1988), 122.

17. Heath McCoy, "Hobbema Homies," March 30, 2002, *Calgary Herald*, Arts & Style section.

18. Gary Elaschuk, "Shooting Straight from the Hip," August 2002, *Alberta Sweetgrass*.

19. Ontario Federation of Indian Friendship Centres, *Urban Aboriginal Child Poverty: A Status Report on Aboriginal Children and their Families in Ontario*, CRRF Perspectives—Focus on Unequal Access, Spring/Summer 2001.

20. Larry K. Brendtro, Martin Brokenleg, and Steve Van Bockern, *Reclaiming Youth at Risk* (Bloomington, IN: National Educational Service, 2002), 45.

21. Fyre Jean Graveline, *Circle Works: Transforming Eurocentric Consciousness* (Halifax, NS: Fernwood Publishing, 1998), 118.

22. Paulo Freire, *Pedagogy of the Oppressed* (New York: Continuum, 1996), 49.

TWO

1. Rupert Ross, *Dancing with a Ghost: Exploring Indian Reality* (Markham, ON: Octopus Publishing Group, 1991), 4.

2. Jeanette Armstrong and Roxana Ng, "Deconstructing Race, Deconstructing Racism," in *Situating "Race" and Racisms in Space, Time, and Theory* (Montreal: McGill-Queen's University Press, 2005), 31.

3. S. Kubish, "Cardinal Knowledge," *New Trail* 60, 3 (2005): 7.

4. Alberta Learning, *First Nations, Métis and Inuit Education Policy Framework*, Edmonton, AB, 2002.

5. R.J. Hood, "Weaving a World of Respect," in *Voice of the Drum* (Brandon, MB: Kingfisher Publications, 2000), 97.

6. Ibid.

THREE

1. Evelyn Lau, *Runaway: Diary of a Street Kid* (Toronto: ON: HarperCollins Publishers Ltd., 1989), 266.
2. Beverly Tatum, "Lighting Candles in the Dark: One Black Woman's Response to White Antiracist Narratives," in *Becoming and Unbecoming White: Owning and Disowning a Racial Identity* (Westport, CT: Bergin & Garvey, 1999).
3. Paul Willis, *Learning to Labor* (New York: Columbia University Press, 1981).
4. David Wellman, "Transforming Received Categories: Discovering Cross-border Identities and Other Subversive Activities," in *Becoming and Unbecoming White: Owning and Disowning a Racial Identity* (Westport, CT: Bergin & Garvey, 1999).
5. Lois Weis, "Revisiting a 1980s *Moment of Critique*," in *Learning to Labor in New Times* (New York: RoutledgeFalmer, 2004).
6. Lyn Mikel Brown, "White Working-class Girls, Femininities, and the Paradox of Resistance," in *From Subjects to Subjectivities* (New York: New York University Press, 2001).
7. Joan Scott, cited in Linda Nicholson, "Interpreting Gender," in *Social Postmodernism: Beyond Identity Politics* (Cambridge: Cambridge University Press, 1995).
8. Linda Nicholson, "Interpreting Gender," in *Social Postmodernism: Beyond Identity Politics* (Cambridge: Cambridge University Press, 1995), 44.
9. Evelyn Lau, 171.
10. Linda Nicholson, "Interpreting Gender," in *Social Postmodernism: Beyond Identity Politics* (Cambridge: Cambridge University Press, 1995), 41.
11. Ibid.
12. Valerie Walkerdine, Helen Lucey and June Melody, "Growing Up Girl: Psychological Explorations of Gender and Class," in *Off White: Readings on Power, Privilege, and Resistance* (New York: Routledge, 2004).

FOUR

1. Michael W. Apple, *Ideology and Curriculum*, 3rd ed. (New York: RoutledgeFalmer, 2004), 126.
2. Alberta Learning, *Removing Barriers to High School Completion—Final Report*, Edmonton, AB, 2001.
3. Alberta Education, *High School Completion Your Future Starts Here—Summary Report on Alberta Education's High School Completion Symposium*, Edmonton, AB, 2006.
4. Terry Wotherspoon and Bernard Schissel, "The Business of Placing Canadian Children and Youth 'At-Risk,'" *Canadian Journal of Education* 26, 3 (2001): 321–39.

5. Terry Wotherspoon and Bernard Schissel, "The Business of Placing Canadian Children and Youth 'At-Risk,'" *Canadian Journal of Education* 26, 3 (2001): 321–39.

6. Diane Conrad, "Exploring Risky Youth Experiences: Popular Theatre as a Participatory, Performative Research Method [Electronic Version]," *International Journal of Qualitative Methods* 3.

7. Michael W. Apple, *Ideology and Curriculum* 3rd ed. (New York: RoutledgeFalmer, 2004), 126.

8. J. Laddish, "Effects in the Classroom: Some Teacher Views of Program and Funding Changes in Special Education in Alberta" (Unpublished manuscript, University of Alberta, 2002).

9. Alberta Learning, *Special Education Definitions,* 2004.

10. Michael W. Apple, *Ideology and Curriculum* 3rd ed. (New York: RoutledgeFalmer, 2004), 135.

11. Alberta Education, *Alberta Education's Annual Report,* Edmonton, AB, 1999.

12. Alberta Learning, *Removing Barriers to High School Completion—Final Report,* Edmonton, AB, 2001.

FIVE

1. Paulo Freire, *Teachers as Cultural Workers: Letters to Those who Dare Teach,* expanded edition (Cambridge, MA: Westview Press, 2005), 130.

2. For example: Alberta Learning, *Removing Barriers to High School Completion—Final Report,* Edmonton, AB, 2001; M. O'Dowd, "Re-visioning Empowerment with the Research Subject and the 'At-Risk,'" in *Education, Inequality and Social Identity* (Washington, DC: The Falmer Press, 1993), 21–56; Laura Sokal, "Needing to Belong: Networks of Risk and Resilience," in *Resiliency and Capacity Building* (Winnipeg, MB: Portage & Main Press, 2003), 15–32.

3. Alberta Learning, *Removing Barriers to High School Completion—Final Report,* Edmonton, AB, 2001.

4. Augusto Boal, *Theatre of the Oppressed* (New York: Theatre Communications Group, 1985), 125.

5. Tim Prentki and Jan Selman, *Popular Theatre in Political Culture: Britain and Canada in Focus* (Portland, OR: Intellect, 2000), 8.

6. Ibid..

7. Jeanette Armstrong, *Slash* (Penticton, BC: Theytus Books, 1988), 77.

8. Ira Shor, "What is Critical Literacy?" in *Critical Literacy in Action: Writing Words, Changing Worlds* (Portsmouth, NH: Boynton/Cook Publishers, Inc.), 1.

9. Jeanette Armstrong, *Slash* (Penticton, BC: Theytus Books, 1988), 65.

10. Evelyn Lau, *Runaway: Diary of a Street Kid* (Toronto: ON: HarperCollins Publishers Ltd., 1989), 67.

SIX

1. Michael Novak, *Ascent of the Mountain, Flight of the Dove: An Invitation to Religious Studies* (New York: Harper & Row, 1978), 43.
2. Stephen J. Ball, "The Sociology of Education: A Disputational Account," in *The RoutledgeFalmer Reader in Sociology of Education* (London, UK: RoutledgeFalmer, 2004), 1–13.
3. Andy Furlong and Fred Cartmel, *Young People and Social Change: Individualization and Risk in Late Modernity* (Buckingham, UK: Open University Press, 1997), 7.
4. Ibid., 4.
5. Michael W. Apple, "Cultural Politics and the Text," in *The RoutledgeFalmer Reader in Sociology of Education* (London, UK: RoutledgeFalmer, 2004), 179.
6. Pierre Bourdieu, "The Forms of Capital," in *The RoutledgeFalmer Reader in Sociology of Education* (London, UK: RoutledgeFalmer, 2004), 26.

BIBLIOGRAPHY

Alberta Education. *Alberta Education's Annual Report.* Edmonton, 1999.
Alberta Learning. *Removing Barriers to High School Completion—Final Report.*
    Edmonton, 2001.
Alberta Learning. *Special Education Definitions.* Edmonton, 2004.
Anderson, K. *A Recognition of Being.* Toronto, ON: Sumach Press, 2000.
Apple, M.W. "Cultural Politics and the Text." In S.J. Ball, ed. *The*
    RoutledgeFalmer Reader in Sociology of Education. (179–95). London, UK:
    RoutledgeFalmer, 2004.
Apple, M.W. *Ideology and Curriculum.* New York: RoutledgeFalmer, 2004.
Armstrong, J. *Slash.* Penticton, BC: Theytus Books, 1988.
Ball, S.J. "The Sociology of Education: A Disputational Account." In S.J. Ball, ed.
    The RoutledgeFalmer Reader in Sociology of Education. (1–13). London, UK:
    RoutledgeFalmer, 2004.
Battiste, M., & Henderson, J.Y. *Protecting Indigenous Knowledge and Heritage.*
    Saskatoon, SK: Purich Publishing Ltd., 2000.
Boal, A. *Theatre of the Oppressed.* New York: Theatre Communications Group,
    1985.
Bourdieu, P. "The Forms of Capital." In S.J. Ball, ed. *The RoutledgeFalmer Reader*
    in Sociology of Education. (15–29). London, UK: RoutledgeFalmer, 2004.
Brendtro, L.K., Brokenleg, M., & Van Bockern, S. *Reclaiming Youth At Risk.*
    Bloomington, IN: National Educational Service, 2002.
Brown, L.M. "White working class girls, femininities, and the paradox of
    resistance." In. D.L. Tolman & M. Brydon-Miller, eds. *From Subjects to*
    Subjectivities. (95–110). New York: New York University Press, 2001.
Brown, S. *Words in the Wilderness: Critical Literacy in the Borderlands.* Albany,
    NY: State University of New York Press, 2000.
Cloutier, J. "Joe Cloutier, Founder of Inner City Drama & Inner City High
    School." *The Source* 7(3), 12–13. 2002.
Cloutier, J. "Upgrading your Future." *Beat the Street,* 2–3. 2005.
Conrad, D. (2004). "Exploring risky youth experiences: Popular theatre as
    a participatory, performative research method." *International Journal*
    of Qualitative Methods 3 (1). Artcle 2. Retrieved from
    http://www.ualberta.ca/~iiqm/backissues/3_1/html/conrad.html

Dalgetty, A. *Inner City High School Literacy Program*. Unpublished manuscript. 2003.

Dalgetty, A., & Cloutier, J. "Popular Theatre, Cultural Awareness and Solidarity: Canada to Nicaragua." In T. Prentki & J. Selman, eds. *Popular Theatre in Political Culture*. (42–47). Portland, OR: Intellect Books, 2000.

Duncan-Andrade, J. "Urban Youth, Media Literacy, and Increased Critical Civic Participation." In *Youth, Communities, and Social Justice*. New York: Routledge, 2006.

Dyson, M.E. *Holler if You Hear Me: Searching for Tupac Shakur*. New York: Basic Civitas Books, 2001.

Freire, P. *Pedagogy of the Oppressed*. New York: Continuum, 1996.

Furlong, A., & Cartmel, F. *Young People and Social Change: Individualization and Risk in Late Modernity*. Buckingham, UK: Open University Press, 1997.

Gadamer. H.-G. *Truth and Method*. New York: Continuum, 1989.

Gamoran, A. "High Standards: A Strategy for Equalizing Opportunities to Learn?" In R.D. Kahlenberg, ed. *A Notion At Risk*. New York: The Century Foundation Press, 2000.

Giroux, H.A. *Teachers as Intellectuals: Toward a Critical Pedagogy of Learning*. Granby, MA: Bergin & Garvey, 1988.

Gore, J.M. *The Struggle for Pedagogies*. New York: Routledge, 1993.

Graveline, F.J. *Circle Works: Transforming Eurocentric Consciousness*. Halifax: Fernwood Publishing, 1998.

Hall, S. "New Ethnicities." In D. Morley & K.-H. Chen, eds. *Stuart Hall: Critical Dialogues in Cultural Studies*. (441–49). London, UK: Routledge, 1996.

Hoikkala, P. "Feminists or Reformers? American Indian Women and Community in Phoenix, 1965–1980." In S. Lobo & K. Peters, eds. *American Indians and the Urban Experience*. (127–46). Walnut Creek, CA: AltaMira Press, 2001.

Hood, R.J. "Weaving a World of Respect." In R. Neil, ed. *Voice of the Drum: Indigenous Education and Culture*. (81–100). Brandon, MB: Kingfisher Publications, 2000.

Kubish, S. "Cardinal Knowledge." *New Trail* 60 (3), 7. 2005.

Laddish, J. *Effects in the Classroom: Some Teacher Views of Program and Funding Changes in Special Education in Alberta*. Unpublished manuscript, University of Alberta. 2002.

Lau, E. *Runaway: Diary of a Street Kid*. Toronto, ON: HarperCollins Publishers Ltd., 1989.

Lewis, M. "Interrupting Patriarchy: Politics, Resistance, and Transformation in the Feminist Classroom." In I. Shor & C. Pari, eds. *Education is Politics: Critical Teaching across Differences, Postsecondary*. (82–106). Portsmouth, NH: Boynton/Cook Publishers, Inc., 2000.

Mah, B. "Listen to the Children: They Don't Think They're Safe." *Edmonton Journal*. A1, A14. January 24, 2001.

McCoy, H. "Hobbema Homies." *Calgary Herald*. March 30, 2002.

Mohanty, C.T. "Feminist Encounters: Locating the Politics of Experience." In L. Nicholson & S. Seidman, eds. *Social Postmodernism: Beyond Identity Politics.* (68–86). Cambridge: Cambridge University Press, 1995.

Nicholson, L., & Seidman, S. "Introduction." In L. Nicholson & S. Seidman, eds. *Social Postmodernism: Beyond Identity Politics.* (1–38). Cambridge: Cambridge University Press, 1995.

Novak, M. *Ascent of the Mountain, Flight of the Dove: An Invitation to Religious Studies.* New York: Harper & Row, 1978.

O'Dowd, M. "Re-visioning Empowerment with the Research Subject and the 'At-risk.'" In L. Angus, ed. *Education, Inequality and Social Identity.* (21–56). Washington, DC: The Falmer Press, 1993.

Organisation for Economic Co-operation and Development. *Our Children at Risk.* Paris: Centre for Educational Research and Innovation, 1995.

Prentki, T., & Selman, J. *Popular Theatre in Political Culture: Britain and Canada in Focus.* Portland, OR: Intellect, 2000.

Reay, D. "Finding or Losing Yourself?" In S.J. Ball, ed. *The RoutledgeFalmer Reader in Sociology of Education.* (30–44). London, UK: RoutledgeFalmer, 2004.

Rosenthal, R. "Feminists in Action: How to Practice What We Teach." In I. Shor & C. Pari, eds. *Education is Politics: Critical Teaching Across Differences, Postsecondary.* (107–23). Portsmouth, NH: Boynton/Cook Publishers, Inc., 2000.

Ross, R. *Dancing With a Ghost.* Markham, ON: Octopus Publishing Group, 1991.

Shakur, T. *The Rose that Grew from Concrete.* New York: Pocket Books, 1999.

Shor, I. "What is Critical Literacy?" In I. Shor & C. Pari, eds. *Critical Literacy in Action: Writing Words, Changing Worlds.* (1–30). Portsmouth, NH: Boynton/Cook Publishers, Inc., 1999.

Smith, D.G. "Hermeneutic Inquiry: The Hermeneutic Imagination and the Pedagogic Text." In E.C. Short, ed. *Forms of Curriculum Inquiry.* (187–209). Albany, NY: State University of New York Press, 1991.

Tatum, B.D. "Lighting Candles in the Dark: One Black Woman's Response to White Antiracist Narratives." In C. Clark & J. O'Donnell, eds. *Becoming and Unbecoming White: Owning and Disowning a Racial Identity.* (56–63). Westport, CT: Bergin & Garvey, 1999.

Walkerdine, V., Lucey, H., & Melody, J. "Growing Up Girl: Psychosocial Explorations of Gender and Class." In M. Fine, L. Weis, L. Pruitt, & A. Burns, eds. *Off White: Readings on Power, Privilege, and Resistance.* (98–113). New York: Routledge, 2004.

Weis, L. "Revisiting a 1980s 'Moment of Critique.'" In N. Dolby & G. Dimitriadis, eds. *Learning to Labor in New Times.* (111–32). New York: RoutledgeFalmer, 2004.

Wellman, D. "Transforming Received Categories: Discovering Cross-border Identities and Other Subversive Activities." In C. Clark & J. O'Donnell, eds. *Becoming and Unbecoming White: Owning and Disowning a Racial Identity.* (78–91). Westport, CT: Bergin & Garvey, 1999.

Willis, P. *Learning to Labor.* New York: Columbia University Press, 1981.

Wishart Leard, D., & Linden, N. *Inner City Youth, Schooling, and Mental Health.* Paper presented at the annual meeting of Canadian Mental Health Association, Edmonton, AB, 2005.

Wotherspoon, T. and B. Schissel. "The Business of Placing Canadian Children and Youth 'At-risk.'" *Canadian Journal of Education* 26(3), 321–339. 2001.

INDEX

Sara's feelings on, 70–71
See also labelling illiteracy, 120
inner city
    and feeling of danger, 59–60
    and public school, 67–68
    and survival skills, 38–39
    volunteer experience in, 31–32
in-service training, 114
integrated education programs, 47,
    49–50, 51–56, 138

James (teacher)
    and acceptance of Aboriginals as
        individuals, 46
    and class distinctions, 52
    and communication between staff
        and students, 110, 115
    and flexibility, 14, 26
    and labelling students, 94, 95
    and new teachers, 106, 107–08
    and public school, 18
    and student motivation, 4–5
    and student skills, 38–39, 100
    and students' sense of ownership,
        114–15, 117, 118
    and students as victims, 19
    and study of art, 121, 122
    and teaching styles, 6, 106
    and teaching values, 11, 102
    and traditional teacher training, 21
    as trusted teacher, 28
    and WRS process, 35, 117–18, 125
job security, 113
Joel (student), 2, 62, 63

Kelsey (student)
    and public school, 62–63, 66–67,
        82–83
    on race at WRS, 79–80
    on relationship of trust with
        teachers, 28, 29
Kevin (student), 17, 35–36, 62, 111
Kristine (teacher)
    and art classes, 30, 120
    and bridging courses, 20
    excitement over students, 114, 116
    and measures of success, 119
    and new teachers, 39
    and self-directed learning, 25–26

and sharing circles, 111
as trusted teacher, 28

labelling
    by Alberta Education, 99–100
    "at-risk" students, 96–98, 101–02
    danger of, 94–96, 140
    and definitions, xvi–xvii
    and hiding individuals, 90–91
    and politics of literacy, 126, 129–30
    See also identity
Lau, Evelyn, 15, 86–87, 129
Leonard (youth worker)
    and building trust, 27, 115
    and cross-cultural awareness,
        12, 35
    and gender, 84–85
    on his identity, 58, 61
    and life's choices, 123
    on poverty, 32, 59–60
    and racial attitudes, 13, 54–55
    and segregated courses, 51, 53
    and students' sense of success,
        26, 116, 122
    on Transition Year Program at
        U of Alberta, 48–49
    and WRS support, 17

manipulation, 14, 107
margins/marginalization, 139
Meg (teacher)
    adapting to WRS, 24, 25, 103
    and classroom environment, 6
    and openness, 112–13
    and senior WRS courses, 125
    and staff meetings, 107
    and teaching styles, 3
    and use of labels, 94–95
    and WRS students, 4, 8
mentoring, 113–14
Morales, Agustin Sapon, 62, 63
motherhood, 7–8, 9–10
motivation, 4–5, 103

new teachers
    difficulty fitting in at WRS, 21,
        24–25, 102–04, 106–08
    and lack of job security, 113

159

THE ROSE THAT GREW FROM CONCRETE

161